"Do not fear mistakes.
Wisdom is often born of
such mistakes.
You will know failure.
Determine now to acquire
the confidence required
to overcome it.
Reach out..."

Paul V. Galvin

The Founder's Touch

LIMITED EDITION

THE FOUNDER'S TOUCH

The Life of Paul Galvin of Motorola

by
Harry Mark Petrakis

McGRAW-HILL BOOK COMPANY
New York
Toronto
London

923.8
G~P

THE FOUNDER'S TOUCH:
The Life of Paul Galvin of Motorola

Contents

Introduction

In 1959, Paul Galvin's family persuaded him to start narrating and recording some of his early childhood and business experiences. He barely got started before his death in November of that year. These tape recordings formed the starting point of this book. It was through them that I was first introduced to him.

I never knew Paul Galvin personally. I am sorry that I did not have the chance to know him and talk to him, for biography is a tenuous art. It calls upon the biographer to return the very breath of life to the memories, recollections, letters, snatches of film and photographs which seem to be all that survive a man's stay on this earth.

Henry James wrote very truly of the change that takes place between the moment when a man is alive and that period beginning with his death: "Those in whose regard he has held a high place find his image strangely simplified and summarized. The figure retained by memory is compressed and intensified; accidents have dropped away from it and shades have ceased to count; it stands, sharply, for a few esteemed and cherished things."

The relevance of this analysis was borne out when in a series of interviews a strong bright image of Paul Galvin was what remained.

He founded a little company and guided its destiny as it grew. He was never a dehumanized figure of "the boss" but all of his life remained remarkably accessible to his people. He had no

titan's urge for solitude. He was not merely a
dreamer but a worker in a way that isn't fashionable any more. He was not an engineer but a salesman, not an inventor but a builder whose blue-
prints were people.

He was a man of medium height, never overly
strong physically, but giving the impression of
great strength. His conversation had a pictur-
esque bite to it; he was almost a grass-roots poet
in his ability to color a phrase. "There he sits,"
he said of one of his executives who had earned
his displeasure, "listening to his arteries harden."

In his telephone conversations with associates, his resonant voice seemed to overflow the
receiver at the other end. He was a religious man
who lived devotedly by his faith and yet he was
not above small infractions. He quite often used
profanity. But he was simply using words that
gave what he thought was the proper impact and
emphasis to his expressions.

He had a fierce conviction all of his life that
everything would be all right, "if we just keep in
motion." He would stress this constantly to his
executives, an undertone of energy evident in his
voice and in the eloquent way he used his hands.

Yet for all his emphasis on motion he could
always spare the time to sit quietly with an old
employee, questioning him about a family illness
or some personal problem.

He had a canny insight and perception about
people and events and yet there were times when

these were blunted by his obstinacy. But when someone stood up to him and explained the facts, he candidly acknowledged his mistake.

When he appointed his son, Bob, to the position of President of Motorola, he spoke to a group including his plant foremen about the appointment. At the finish he told them with finality: "I am still the boss here. If there is any question about that, just meet me in the parking lot after hours and I'll take on any two of you to prove it." He could not have handled one of the brawny shop foremen, let alone two, but because of the great affection and respect they had for him, they wanted to believe that he could.

That kind of affection and respect never really allows the memory of a man to die. Those who worked with him will always remember him arguing and fussing, correcting and encouraging, counseling and consoling.

The term by which he is most often described by his associates and his competitors is that he was "just." It is an abused word that has been drained of much of its vitality and meaning. But Paul Galvin lived justly and practiced justice with an unusual grace.

This is his story.

Galvin's
Harvard
1

Paul Galvin was born in a small midwestern town, Harvard, Illinois, on June 29, 1895. His people were Irish, of sturdy pioneer stock, and they lived, raised their children, and died in Harvard.

Harvard is in the northern end of McHenry County, about 50 miles from the Wisconsin state line. In the middle of the nineteenth century, when the town was plotted, the country around it had been a series of scattered trails and rolling prairies. The immigrants and the sons of immigrants began to settle there with the cessation of the Civil and the Indian Wars. The Chicago and North Western Railroad brought a brief boom to the town with its arrival in 1856 and for a while made Harvard a pivotal rail center. It is now the junction point for two branches of the line, one of the many small midwestern towns served by the C & NW.

The countryside around the town is the flat prairie land of the middle west, broken here and there by a rise of hill and a grove of trees. In the autumn the woods were burnished the colors of scarlet and gold. The quail and the prairie hens nestled beneath the shadow of the elms and the oaks. The fields were alive with rabbits, the bushes heavy with berries.

In the winter, the gray heavy skies seemed to touch the very roofs of the houses and barns and the snow fell and seemed to give the earth a flawless serenity.

1

But the town itself, as with so many other small towns at the turn of the century, was a rude and unlovely settlement of scattered buildings beside roads that were muddy in the spring and frozen into the ruts of wagon wheels in the winter.

If it is true that Emerson's Concord and Lincoln's Springfield helped define the visions that shaped the men, it is also true that for many Americans in the early years of this century the small town did much to define and foster a certain energy and character. And the small midwestern town had a special place in this development.

The vitality of the Midwest was the vitality of the frontier pushing savagely into the wilderness. There were no great ruling families such as those of New England—no Adams and Lowells and Holmes to provide leadership—but traders and hunters, gamblers and adventurers, goaded by the splendor and wealth of a land teeming with resources. A short way behind them came the home seekers and the farmers to share the turbulent life, restless swarms of men and women from the more settled east moving into the land between the Appalachians and the Mississippi. Their settlements dotted the land and the ground was tilled and houses built of log and frame and the towns were born.

All his life the views of Paul Galvin essentially reflected the direct, no-nonsense philosophy of his small town heritage. His own personality, friendly, yet with a certain reserve, salty, yet at times very gentle, his stress on personal loyalties, his shrewd assessment of men and his strong moral code was an expression of what was most durable in the values of the small town.

But the passing years have witnessed the diluting of the frontier tradition and the loss of much of the vigor. The insulation of the small town has succumbed before the supermarket and the automobile, the radio and TV, the impact of urban culture.

Today, Harvard, like many other small towns in a society in transition, is a sort of balance wheel between the farm and the city. It still retains some of the values that belong to the land and for its older residents a sense of heritage and tradition.

"A man has got anything he wants right here," an old resident of Harvard says. "I was born here and one of these days I'll die in Harvard." But he is forced to admit a little sadly that, "very few of the kids ever come back here to live after they've gone away to school or to work."

This much is true. The pace of living in the small town is less frantic than it is in the big city. There is still a willingness to meet people openly, to think of them more easily as neighbors and friends. But the tempo of the small town beats with a rhythm that is mostly for older ears, for those who choose stubbornly to remain, a rhythm that many of the young people ignore or do not hear.

"Let them go," Galvin would say. "If they can't find what they want at home, let them go."

From his own boyhood he understood that beyond the borders of any small town is the vision of the city. He remembered his own yearnings and dreams and sympathized with the young who felt the tranquility of the small town was stagnant, the unity with the land was useless, and their identity as individuals something they had to discover away from their own hearth.

On his maternal side, Paul Galvin's grandfather was a farmer named William Brickley. He had given up farming when he married his wife, Mary Ann, and moved into Harvard where for the remainder of his life he worked as a flagman on the C & NW. They had four children (the youngest was Alice Brickley, Paul Galvin's mother).

There is a fading photograph of William Brickley among the family papers showing a fierce-eyed and wiry-bodied old patriarch surrounded by a dozen of his grandchildren, all under the stern shadow of his great white handlebar mustache.

Grandmother Brickley is remembered by her grandchildren as a soft-spoken and unselfish woman, never raising her voice in anger or her hand except to greet or caress one of the children.

Paul Galvin had no recollection of his paternal grandfather. He was also a farmer of Irish stock who worked hard and died young leaving a wife and nine children. (His son, John Galvin, was the father of Paul Galvin.)

Grandpa Galvin's widow, who survived him by almost twenty years, was an imposing matriarch of a woman. A photograph of her taken in the last decade of her life shows her posing in the characteristic black taffeta trimmed with lace. Her gray hair coiled firmly into a bun is parted sharply in the middle and her lips are shaped to a single stern line. As a young girl she had crossed the continent by covered wagon to California and then returned to Illinois. She had survived wild Indian raids and the other hardships of the journeys. There was pioneer iron in the way she walked and talked. She is remembered vividly by her grandchildren for the black starched dresses that rustled as she walked, for her wonderful stories, and for the cane that she used to poke them with when she was displeased.

In her last years, with her children grown and married and scattered across the world, Grandma Galvin settled down in Harvard in a white clapboard house beside the house of the Brickley grandparents. In her kitchen, which caught the golden rays of the afternoon sun, the grandmothers would sit together and sip their tea.

John Galvin and Alice Brickley, the parents of Paul, Raymond, Joseph, Philip, and an only daughter, Helen, were married on January 31,

1894. Paul, the eldest of their children, was born the following year.

John Galvin had tried farming for a while but found the life too hard and lonely and moved his family into Harvard where he opened a saloon. Photographs of him taken in those early years show a husky, strongly built man, taller than any of his sons would grow to be, wearing a jaunty derby on his thick black curly hair. There was a good deal of an Irish sport about him, and a streak of instability in economic matters. He was lively and spirited with considerable wit. He worked diligently and thanked God in his prayers for his prosperity. No tyrant, he was convinced of what was right and wrong and brought up his children to toe that mark. His patrons in the saloon were the townsmen and farmers who came in to trade and shop.

John Galvin was respected by them, not only for his temper and strong arm which could quickly heave a rowdy into the street, but for his generosity. He was, above all, a warm and gregarious man who enjoyed the boisterous company of men.

But Alice Galvin, the wife and mother, embodied the heart of their house. She was a lovely woman with a great dignity and grace. A love of God and reverence for His works set the pattern of her life. She was strengthened by the love of her children and her husband's devotion. Caring a great deal for him, she was content to allow the reins of decision to remain in his hands, but in certain crises which directly threatened the welfare of the family she would not yield.

With his volatile nature, John Galvin was sometimes given to impulsive enthusiams and one such instance, in the first years after they had settled in Harvard, involved a contemplated second move to some backwoods country store. Alice Galvin had known the desolate life of the farm and she did not want her children moved away from Harvard. She challenged her husband in this move and Paul, her eldest son, was her ally. With what must have been some bitterness, John Galvin, sensing some immovable will in her, gave ground. But for the most part these instances of friction were very rare and the house full of growing children had a happy turbulence.

"The mother in the small town of those days was always closer to the children," Paul Galvin was to recall later. "This was not only in Harvard—but I think you would find it in every small town. The man worked through his day, came home and ate supper and afterwards went back uptown to the tobacco shop or the newsstand where he cronied with his friends and the farmers who came in and exchanged gossip with the villagers till about ten o'clock. But it was a congregation of men. Each mother was home doing the dishes. When she got through, she maybe would sit down in her rocker or visit another lady close by. If it was wintertime and the father didn't go out, he'd read the paper or he'd read a book. The mother got the kids to bed, and if they had to take some goose oil for a cold the mother saw to that.

"There were things we did together as a family in the evening. I think we were among the first in town to have a phonograph with a great big morning-glory horn. We had a player piano equipped with a paper roll with holes in it and we would pump it and get 'Sweet Adeline' or one of the other songs of the day. We had a lantern with slides that we would project on a sheet suspended in the kitchen.

"In the summertime our evenings were spent outdoors. The kids gathered, we had band concerts, bought ice cream cones, and we pulled the hair ribbons of the girls. We would have games on nights the band didn't play, games like 'Run Sheep Run,' 'Kick the Can,' 'Pom Pom Pull Away'—games of a nature that I guess kids were playing everywhere."

Paul Galvin at that time was about ten years old, a fine-boned boy with luminous eyes and a mouth a little too wide for his face. Perhaps, because he was the eldest of five children with more expected of him, there was an overtone of seriousness about him. A part of him did not seem completely a child but almost a miniature adult with an awareness of the furies of the adult world.

He was fiercely protective of his younger brothers and sister. Trying to set a standard for them, he drove himself hard. He could also be protective of his friends. This was reflected in an episode that involved the father of one of the boys in the town.

"Someone had either kicked or hit his son," Paul Galvin recalled. "This boy went home and complained to his father. A group of us were sitting along the stone curbing when this father came around and grabbed the first kid in our group and started to give him an unmerciful beating. No explanation at all, he just pounded hell out of the kid. Well, this got us mad, and we had him arrested. Then we sought out the most important lawyer in Harvard—there were only two— and we gave him our case. I think the lawyer took it in fun as much as anything else. The fellow we had arrested got the other attorney and we had a trial with witnesses. The trial was scheduled before my father found out. This man was a three-door neighbor from where we lived. I don't remember my father or any of the other parents making a great fuss about it. I think basically the families thought it shouldn't take place, but they left us alone.

"It turned out this trial was held on two of the most important days of the annual county fair and that put us out of the fair but we stuck to our guns. One of the things that bothered us was that these two lawyers would go out to lunch with their arms practically around each other's shoulders. We thought they were supposed to be as irate as we were. But the net of it was that this fellow was found guilty and fined $2 and court costs which amounted to about $3.75 or something like that. We won the case and then had to pay our lawyer the $10 that he charged us.''

Reflecting on this experience in his later years, Galvin remained sensitive to any move by some person or company to ''push him around.'' His first reaction was that most differences could be settled by a meeting of principals acting in good faith. When these efforts failed, he believed in recourse to the law. A measure of his success was that throughout his life he fought very few business battles in a court of law.

"If You're Going to Take a Licking ... Take It"

2

Excitement such as the trial was rare. Most of the time the days were spent in the unhurried pattern of small town life. In the summer, after their assigned chores were done in the morning, and after a breakfast of wheatcakes and maple syrup, the boys hiked down to the station to watch the trains come in or dropped by the livery stable or played baseball on the prairie outside of town.

Sometimes the group went swimming, but Galvin never went into the water as the result of nearly having drowned when he was six.

"I went swimming with a bunch of kids who were older than I was in the old muddy creek like you'd find in any country farming area—probably the cows used it when we weren't there. The older fellows would let us dive or jump off their backs. I jumped off one of these boys and somebody else dove off the other side of the creek and we collided. It knocked me out and I didn't know what was happening until I was out on the bank and they were rolling me over a log.

"After that experience I never was able to fathom the idea of getting into water over my head. We lived only twenty-one miles from Lake Geneva, Wisconsin, and most kids my age went up there and learned to be good swimmers. We'd go on camping trips with these fellows and take a horse and buggy and a tent into the forest near the lake and do our own cooking, and things like that. I could do all the other things but I couldn't swim."

11

Often Sunday afternoons the Galvin children walked to their grandparents' home. The stiffly posed photographs of this period show Galvin and his brothers and sister as they looked on these family excursions. The high, white collars of the boys were buttoned as tight as nooses around their throats and their hair was slicked down and parted in a sharp pale line down the middle. Helen Galvin wore a lacy flounced dress with decorative little ribbons in her hair.

Grandmother Galvin would sit with the somber majesty of a Victoria in her parlor with the children gathered around her knees while she told them again of the wild Indian raids against the wagon train.

Another of the favorite visits for the children was to carry a warm supper down to Grandpa Brickley who was a flagman on the railroad. The lighting of the stove in his shanty for the first time in the autumn was a ritual the children loved. Then, during some of the long winter evenings, they sat huddled around the stove listening to the wind rattle the windows and hearing the long eerie whistle of the trains in the night.

These two threads of experience must have had their firming influence in the development of Galvin's character. He would remember and speak of them all his life. He was at first hand able to absorb from his pioneer grandmother the legend of the vital tradition, the courage of the men and women in the face of hardship and danger. From his flagman grandfather and the many hours in the shanty there must have come a sense of the movement of the great trains crossing the continent, of the rhythm of a nation of people never content to remain still. This sense of tradition and movement was to affect his thinking in his business activities.

His son, Bob, in early memories of his father recalled a journey they made together by car, train, plane and boat all on the same trip. And as a child in family parties, Bob remembered people danced or played games but never just sat around. In later years, Galvin stressed that one mark of a good executive was that he keep moving. And toward the end of his life, ill and close to death, Galvin told his good friend Matt Hickey that in his restless sleep at night he had dreams of furiously pedaling a bicycle so that in the morning he woke weary and exhausted as if he had been racing all night long.

When Galvin was eleven, he got his first job stripping the stems from large tobacco leaves for a small tobacco factory in the town. He got $2 a week during vacation for working from 7 A.M. to 6 P.M. six days a week. He continued this job for two summers.

"Until I was thirteen in 1908, I was taking some after-school work to make up time lost as a result of an appendicitis operation.

"Mrs. Webster was the teacher I liked best. She was one of these 'solid-rock' English ladies who had tremendous capability. She was a fine teacher and apparently she must have seen something in me that other people didn't think worth bothering about. She encouraged me to become interested in business.

"Her interest stimulated me into looking around for an opportunity to enter business. About this time I observed a couple of brothers in the popcorn business. Harvard at that time was a junction point, not a division point. The trains stopped so they could be serviced, maybe an average of seven minutes. These boys were selling popcorn at the trains, and without any license or permission from them I projected myself into this business.

"I guess that for the first time I experienced the struggle of free enterprise. The original group never accepted the fact that anybody else had a right in their territory. And so war broke out.

"We had just a wicker basket—an ordinary market basket—we stacked twenty bags of popcorn in it, and if somebody came along and kicked that basket, our twenty bags of popcorn were all over the place. Well, this war got to the point where older boys were hired to do some of the fighting. Of course, this was all among kids—none of us were more than fifteen years old—but you could see a kind of jungle law working anyhow. After awhile we had some meetings and called the war off because if we kept it up nobody would be in business."

With the warfare between the young groups of popcorn salesmen over, a period of expansion set in. Galvin sought various means of increasing sales.

"In the summer time I made a popcorn stand and wheeled it up to town, and in addition to selling popcorn at the trains, I sold it on Main Street. In the winter time I would pop the corn on our cook stove at home that was fired with hard coal. My mother would get these coals red hot by the time I came home from school, and would give me an opportunity to pop enough for about twenty bags of corn at a time. I would proceed up to the depot which was three blocks away and hang around till the trains came in. I would sell what I could and then come home for supper and go back after supper with a fresh batch. I kept that up for all the winter.

"I advertised hot buttered popcorn, and if most of the time it wasn't hot it would have lots of butter and salt. I would try to keep it as warm as possible in some little place around the yards like Grandpa Brickley's shanty. After I finished with the trains, I would wheel my stand on the street for the rest of the evening. My brothers Raymond (Burley) and Joe worked with me as the business grew. Harvard was a trading town and a farmer's center, comprised of two important blocks and we had a good location where people gathered. The

following season I built another stand and put
that on the corner of the second best block and
Burley worked that one.

"After awhile Burley and Joe worked the
stands and I handled the trains, because that involved the hopping on and the hopping off of cars.
If you didn't make it off in time the train carried
you to the next station which was Beloit, Wisconsin. That was a long haul back. I never got
carried away to Beloit, but I had to hop off in the
yards quite often after the train had started."

It was a profitable business for the Galvin
boys which they continued after school and after
supper each evening as the winter descended and
the wind blew colder.

When the big snow of 1910 hit Harvard, the
boys with the assistance of their mother packaged
several large baskets full of ham sandwiches and
took them down to sell to the passengers on the
snowed-in trains.

"I remember we had six or seven trains
backed up for miles into town. There were people
on them and although they had heat because they
had steam engines, they had no food. We dropped
the popcorn business for the moment, cut school
for a couple of days, and made ham sandwiches.
There was no butter on them because we didn't
have time to butter them, but we had a bonanza
with our sandwiches. We would have to walk a
mile or two to get to these marooned trains and as
soon as we got into a car we were stormed by the

hungry passengers. We could probably have sold them for a quarter but selling them at ten cents made us a fair profit.''

The boys spent each hour before going to bed jubilantly adding up their profits at the kitchen table. Then the plows got through, the trains started away and the great sandwich boom of 1910 departed with them. Years later in January of 1918 in a letter to his mother from Camp Bowie, Texas after reading of a ferocious blizzard back in the Midwest, Galvin wistfully wrote:

"I wonder who's coining the dough on ham sandwiches this snow—remember?''

When summer came Galvin introduced a new product.

"We got the idea we could start selling ice cream cones at the trains. We dreamed up a special tray—a little half-moon affair that we would strap onto our body and in the middle was a little opening where we kept about a half gallon of ice cream in ice. On the sides, we cut holes where we would pile up the cones. And we went onto the trains selling fresh ice cream cones. We'd do this only in the summer time, although the popcorn was a year around affair. But back in the days where there was no air conditioning and the trains were wide open, full of smoke and cinders, ice cream was a pretty good seller.''

By this time the competition on the trains had become a frenzied horde. Every boy in town wanted to get into the business, and in other

towns along the line groups of boys assaulted the
trains. In Woodstock, the county seat, Charlie
Green, who would grow up to become Galvin's
close friend and attorney, was skimming the
cream of the trade off the trains from Chicago
before they got to Harvard. In Harvard it became
so turbulent that the first boys on were the only
ones who made sales, and the competition to be the
first ones in the cars caused boys to swarm onto the
trains even before they had stopped. One day one
of the boys slipped and fell under the rolling
wheels of a car. He was able to hang on to a rail-
ing and haul himself clear of the wheels until the
train had ground to a stop.

"There was a lot of commotion. People on
the platform squealing and hollering. The station
master's attention was brought to it, and that
ended all train business for everybody. In fact I
had departed already and was two blocks away
before the station master got over there. I knew
that we were out of the popcorn business before
we got the declaration."

In later years Galvin would retell this story
to make a point to his associates when some product or market was on its way out. "Recognize
the signs," he would say. "If you're going to take
a licking, take it, and get on to the next job."

"Strong Reason Is
the Strength of Man"
3

With his concentration no longer diverted to
the selling of popcorn and ice cream, Galvin's
school work improved, and he had a little time for
the social side of high school. Mrs. Webster continued to counsel him of the need to continue his
education in college.

About this time Galvin met the girl he would
marry. Lillian Guinan attended Harvard High
School, a pretty and vivacious girl who appealed
greatly to the young, serious boy. They met for a
few casual dates that involved listening to the
band. She did not play the coquette with him,
and he was impressed by the fact that when he
came calling for her at her grandmother and
grandfather Duggan's house a short distance outside Harvard, she never kept him waiting, but was
always dressed and ready.

Galvin was to occasionally take out another
girl, but during the next few years that carried
him through high school and two years at the University of Illinois and then service in the army, he
kept writing and returning to Lillian. In letters
written to his father and mother when he was in
France in 1918, he mentioned fruit cakes and
cookies sent to him by Lillian and once added the
reverent postscript, "How that girl can bake!"

Although not an overly big youth, his spirit
more than made up for his size. In his Senior
year, he became captain of the football team and
the entire family rejoiced in expectation of a
record breaking season of victories.

19

The Harvard High team under Galvin's leadership trained hard, played hard, but all that season did not manage to win a single game. He took what consolation he could in sipping soft drinks with Lillian.

He also played baseball and basketball and was vice president of the school athletic association. In addition to athletics, he had a real ability in administration. The Harvard High School annual, the *Recaller* for 1913, captioned his picture with, "Strong reason is the strength of man."

He was one of the organizers of the school literary society, a very secret organization known as the "TTTT." Members were solemnly pledged not to reveal the meaning which was "Too Tough To Tackle." There is no mention made of whether other members of the Harvard football squad belonged to that society.

Galvin also took a fling at dramatics. And his strong and resonant voice, in later years to resound through the halls of his own company, suited him to the role of villains which he preferred not to play. His great moment of thespian triumph came during the senior play when he played the male lead, "Father Barbeaud," a rich farmer in the play, *Fanchon the Cricket*.

The demise of the popcorn business did not mean the Galvin boys could sit on their hands. Galvin got a job in a clothing store after school and on Saturday afternoons Joe worked in a feed store and Burley worked for a physician taking care of his horse, two cows, and a yard full of chickens. He had to milk the cows, feed the chickens and groom the horse. To enable Burley to finish his chores Galvin and Joe sometimes helped him. The boys grieved in those moments for the comparatively clean days when they sold popcorn.

On weekend evenings, the seniors of Harvard High gathered at each other's homes and danced and sang. In the Galvin house, the player piano was in frequent use with the youngest brother, Philip, and the sister, Helen, allowed to stay up on Friday nights to pump the pedals and help serve the sandwiches, lemonade and taffy.

Helen Galvin, the only girl among four brothers, was bright and attractive and treated with great affection. Her brother, Joe, who went on with Galvin to become one of the founders of Galvin Manufacturing Company, and, later, Motorola, never wrote a letter home without including a special greeting to her at the end. "Hello, pretty."

Philip Galvin, the youngest of the boys, was a sensitive and introspective youth who lived more tenuously in a world of fantasy than any of the rest of the family. He was a tall, good-looking boy with above-average intelligence who had, as a child, suffered a near fatal bout of rheumatic fever. The illness would periodically return to deplete his energy and strength. As if aware that he would someday in the near future be lost to them, he was treated by all the family with a special gentleness.

Galvin felt particularly close to Phil and counseled and protected him. After he had left Harvard for college and the army, he continued to
write to his brother entreating him to keep up his
spirit as if this alone might provide the means to
sustain life. His death would be the first in a series
of tragedies that darkened Galvin's life.

The summer after finishing high school, Galvin got a job as a clerk to the foreman at the railroad roundhouse and taught himself to type.
Lillian and he made the decision to wait until
after he completed college to marry. He worked at
the roundhouse all summer filling out endless
forms, filing, and answering telephones. This did
not prove to be the kind of work he enjoyed, but it
earned him money which he judiciously saved.

In September of 1913, Galvin prepared to
leave for the University of Illinois. On the day of
his departure Burley and Joe helped carry his
bags down the stairs. His mother provided him a
box filled with sandwiches.

At 18 years of age, full of dreams and determination, but a little fearful of the world outside
his town, he was leaving Harvard for the first
time. There was the bittersweet taste of manhood
and uncertainty, the smoky crispness of fall in the
air, the season's early wood fire smoke drifting up
from the neighbors' houses. This was all familiar
to him and it had the comfort and consolation of
familiar things. Conscious of the family watching
him he tried not to reveal his anxiety. When it

came time for him to board the train, he must
have remembered the countless times he had entered the cars to sell popcorn. Now, that part of
his youth was behind him.

Urbana, Illinois was 150 miles away by train
or buggy. For the first time, he entered an environment much more complex than that of the
small high school. The swarms of students in the
classrooms and libraries were strangers to him,
part of a social structure more organized than
any he had known to that time. He was eager to
get on with things, eager to whip through his
studies and get out into the world. But the books
were burdensome and learning did not come easy.

The money that he had so carefully saved
from the popcorn and ice cream ventures in Harvard went at an astonishingly rapid rate. He took
whatever part time jobs he could find. He set up
pins in a local bowling alley and sought to do
some studying between lines. He distributed hand-
bills for a student cleaner.

He lived in a boarding house for a while and
made friends with Vince Sill and Bob Watkins.
He went to a few parties with them but for the
most part avoided dates with girls. Some of this
reluctance was undoubtedly due to his understanding with Lillian, but it was also true that he
seemed to find most girls frivolous.

A part of him seemed to stand back from the
normal buffoonery of freshmen. Although he participated in football scrimmages and once sent a

photo home showing a mass of tangled bodies on a playing field with his proudly scrawled notation, "You can't see me but I am at the bottom," for the most part the postcard photographs he sent home showed him as a spectator at the Illinois football games.

From a position of prominence in his own home town, he was just another country yokel to some of the boys from the big cities who fancied themselves sophisticated. He worked at his studies with all the energy he could muster after his numerous jobs. He was bothered more by bouts of homesickness than he cared to admit. On more than one occasion he wondered if he would not be just as well off back home.

"I miss you all very much," he wrote in one of his letters home that first year. "Sometimes when I am batting my head to memorize axioms for geometry, I look away from my book and think of you gathered in the kitchen laughing as you eat your supper. O my but I miss you all then."

Toward the end of his first year he began to enjoy the discussion of social and economic ideas. He joined the debating society and argued for socialism, military preparedness, and the supplementing and strengthening of the Sherman Antitrust Act, feeling even then that "the labor of a human being is not a commodity or article of commerce." He permitted himself the indulgence of writing some poetry much of which he destroyed at once and some of which he sent to Lillian warning her that it was for her eyes alone. Many years later, preparing for a festive family party at his house on Normandy Place, he would write the invitations in verse himself.

Meanwhile, his savings were being used faster than he had anticipated. He sought another job as a waiter serving dinner in one of the campus sororities. He had not eaten since the night before and when it came time to serve supper he was so stirred by the sight of warm and savory food that he dropped a tray of plates and was at once discharged.

There was also distressing news from home. Harvard, by local option, had voted to go dry the year before and John Galvin had to close the saloon which provided the income on which the family lived. He had worked for a while as night ticket agent on the railroad but found the salary too meager for his family's needs. In a final desperate effort to salvage his failing economic situation, he traded the saloon property and the large family house which had been built for them in more prosperous times for some Wisconsin farm land which turned out to be worthless. And though the family endured the catastrophe without open complaint, it was a period of bitterness and frustration which Galvin, away at school, felt deeply. Struggling to keep ahead of his studies, con-

stantly pressed to make ends meet and aware of
the fact that he might be needed at home, he managed to finish his freshman year.

Meanwhile the summer of 1914 brought war
to Europe.

If there was in the United States in 1914 a
feeling against entanglement in Europe, nowhere
in the country was this attitude more inflexible
than in the Middle West. To an Illinois farmer,
"Europe" was a vague and absurd entity. It was
difficult for an Irishman to think of going to the
aid of England, or for a German storekeeper to
believe the story of Germany as an unscrupulous
monster.

President Wilson sounded the warning signal
of neutrality and the country momentarily agreed.

That summer of 1914 Galvin worked as a mail
carrier in Harvard and in the fall returned to
Urbana. The normal aspects of neutrality were
being furiously debated by the students. The temper of the times was not conducive to study and
contemplation. Galvin felt the war to be distant
and unrelated to the interests of America and yet
he was moved by the massive image of the conflict.

His primary energies went into his work and
his studies and letters to Lillian and to his mother.
He lived frugally and took his morning and evening meals in cheap restaurants, but his money
still seemed to go with incredible speed. The situation back in Harvard continued to be difficult for
the family, who had on Thanksgiving Day of 1914

moved into a stove heated flat. Although nobody wrote asking him for assistance, he felt selfish in denying it to them. On one or two occasions he sent small checks to his mother for her to use for the family, warning her "not to let father know."

He had moods of loneliness and melancholia and looked forward to the summer. His feelings of freedom and exultation were rare because his poverty was always a burden. This was perhaps a part of the reason his schoolwork was not better.

"There are times when I want to throw the whole business up and just come home," he wrote in January 1915. "I reach back toward you all and I know that it is just that I am panicked sometimes by all that I have to do, and want to run. I won't run I promise you, but I will send you all my love and ask that you think of me sometimes as I think of you."

In another letter of his, in February of that year, he wrote, "I took my history final last week and got it back today. God be praised, I passed, but by so narrow a margin even He must not have been sure until the end."

On a few occasions, he managed to steal a few hours from his labors and his studies and joined some of his fellow students in convivial comradeship spiced with drinking and song. For the most part, these sessions passed without incident, except for one fateful evening when a bathtub was dislodged and thrown to the lawn from a second story window. A cloud was cast over all participants, the innocent as well as the guilty, and there were rumblings of possible expulsion which fortunately did not materialize. The episode sobered Galvin and he spurned these excursions for the balance of the semester. He managed to complete another year and then decided not to return to school.

"I just went as far as I could working as much as I could but I wasn't getting out of the school effort what I would have gotten if I had none of this making a living to go through. I cleaned out all my belongings and when I went home to Harvard in the Spring I told my family that I just gave it up."

"Make the World Safe for Democracy"
4

On leaving the university, he went back to the railroad station in Harvard as a clerk. This job lasted until the spring of 1916. Restless in the shadow of the war, he went to Chicago to job hunt and found a spot in the Commonwealth Edison Company as a clerk. During this period, he lived with his aunt Helen and uncle Jack Kehoe in South Chicago.

In late 1916, Congress doubled the regular army and incorporated local national guard units into it. A building program was launched to rapidly expand the merchant fleet. And President Wilson, victorious in his bid for re-election, could say paradoxically of neutrality, "America ought to keep out of this war, at the expense of anything, except this single thing upon which her character and history are founded: her sense of humanity and justice."

Through one of the departments at Commonwealth Edison, Galvin learned of a new officer's training program at Fort Sheridan, the first one of its kind to be organized. His two years in college were sufficient to qualify him. He went into the training program feeling certain that America would be entering the war. The months of newspaper stories had had their effect upon him as well as on much of the country. From the sinking of the Lusitania, the image of the war had altered. A distant and obscurely motivated conflict had become a clearly defined crusade to "rid the

29

world of the barbarous Hun" and "make the world safe for Democracy."

It was true that Galvin and many of the young men of his time were a soul-hungry generation. The words duty, honor, and patriotism had a certain vitality for them. The prospect of adventure, danger, and possible death was fraught with a kind of glory. Their heroes were Frank Merriwell and Horatio Alger, and they went to a war much as young medieval knights embarked upon a sacred quest.

During the first harsh and competitive months at the officer's training school, Galvin's letters were hastily scrawled. He wrote to his mother on May 18, 1917, a few weeks after America had officially entered the war.

"I received your letter yesterday and was glad to hear from you. We are really in the grind now. From 5:00 A.M. till 10:00 P.M. we only have two hours of spare time. This is no sport camp but real work with big letters. But it's o.k. with me. Your loving son, P.V.G."

In August, as the time to mark those who had successfully completed the course and those who failed came closer, his letters took on a tone of anxiety. He wrote his mother on August 10 two brief lines, enclosing a small sealed envelope.

"The camp is still in excitement and worry. Please obey instructions on envelope enclosed. You are on your honor."

The enclosed envelope was marked: "Not to

be opened until 3:00 P.M. Sunday afternoon. This is in trust to you on your honor. P.V.G."

The entire family, including the grandparents Brickley (grandma Galvin had died in 1914) gathered on Sunday afternoon in the Galvin parlor and anxiously waited until exactly three o'clock to open the letter which read:

"Dear Mother: My breast swells and I just burst out all over with pride, joy and happiness. This is the greatest of all days to shine yet in my life. The joy it gives a son to tell a mother to whom I know it will bring pride the news that I have been chosen and sworn to serve God and Country in the great decision which is to come. I thank God for home and that I have conducted myself honorably to Thee."

In a postscript to his father, he wrote:

"I am now a Lieutenant with a task entrusted to me in this great work our Country is about to begin. I want you to share in this result, ever mindful of the whole-hearted assistance you never refused me."

From Fort Sheridan, Galvin was transferred to Camp Grant and given field and artillery training with some training as well in communications. From Camp Grant he was transferred to a Texas-Oklahoma National Guard unit at Camp Bowie, Texas.

Camp Bowie was a massive new installation with part of the camp still under construction. About 10,000 national guardsmen were there al-

ready with 10,000 more recruits to come and 10,000
drafted men to join them later. As part of a great
army being formed, Galvin felt his enthusiasm
growing.

"Oh the dawns are just indescribably beauti-
ful," he wrote home on September 24. "And by
being up every morning before dawn I can see the
very beginning of the splendor."

To his father in a letter of about the same
date, he wrote:

"I never thought I would like this work as
much as I do, but it gives me the science of the
game. There is the necessity of absolute coordina-
tion between artillery and infantry which can only
be brought about by highly organized communications."

And, remembering who he was and where he
had come from:

"If anyone had told me a year ago that today
at 3:50 p.m. I would be down in the back sands of
Texas, up on a washstand, lecturing to a bunch of
the hardest eggs I ever saw in my life on how to
keep clean and sanitary, I would have sent him to
a padded cell."

In a note to his mother on October 2, 1917:

"I have been assigned as a radio officer of the
131st Field Artillery Regiment. Your loving son,
P.V.G."

He did not forget any of the rest of his
family. On Phil's thirteenth birthday, October 21,
he wrote:

"You are now entering the stage of life when man first becomes dependent on himself. You are broad-minded and I am confident that you see far enough ahead to realize that success does not result from trifling. Be ever attendant to Mother and a big brother to Sis."

His mother remained the central receiver for most of his letters and to her he poured out his heart and the countless new experiences that befell him and enlarged his vision of the world and man.

"The camp is guarded and each man on duty walks what is called a post, similar to a beat for a policeman. Some of the posts are long and lonesome and each man must keep walking all the time. This a.m. at 3:30, when I was making a tour of inspection, I came up to one guard and from beyond the hill in the dark I could see he was not walking. For a moment I thought he was sleeping and then I saw he was kneeling and saying his prayers like I never heard them being said before. Poor boy. I was scared to death he would see me and I moved quietly away."

Near the end of January, 1918, Galvin was transferred for nine weeks to Ft. Sill, Oklahoma for advanced artillery training. In his hard work, he felt he was being toughened and prepared and he could write his mother with jubilation:

"I look upon each new task as a fresh fight and I have come to understand that a man must fight as long as he lives. I don't mean get out on

the street and scrap with the neighbors, but I do
mean a fight in exertion to succeed. As you win
one task and tackle the next, then a man is getting
on. God give me strength in this, my mightiest
task, for fight I will.''

The most important events in a soldier's life
are the letters he writes home and the letters he
receives. All his emotions are poured into them.
They are read and reread with endless delight for
they recall the pleasant and warm memories of
home. Galvin was no exception to this rule, and to
a greater degree perhaps than many others, he
poured out the measure of what he was experienc-
ing.

In June, with the news from Europe bleak, he
tried to console his family.

''You spoke of darkness in the papers—don't
be alarmed, Mother. These are anxious days surely,
but we must accept them with calm. A good
businessman does not audit the books and strike
a balance until the end of the season.''

In July 1918, a postcard marked ''Memphis''
let the family know he was moving.

For five or six weeks, there was no word, and
then his first letter arrived from France. When the
censorship was lifted at the end of the war, he
wrote a long fourteen page letter to his family
describing the attack upon their troopships by
German submarines. But, for the moment, with
the responsibility of censoring his own mail, as

well as the mail of his men, he could only write of impressions without military significance.

"I was struck with the first scenes of France. The old straw-roofed houses, narrow cobble-stoned streets, wooden shoes and ox teams. And the thing that astonishes me is that you always see the people who are suffering smiling. The old men and women go about smiling, and even the countless men and women in mourning manage to smile. It is an incredible lesson really to us Americans who wrinkle our brow and scowl at the slightest provocation."

But even in these moments of appraisal and evaluation, he was always thinking of home.

"All the stores remind me of the little millinery shop Mrs. Howe used to run. Remember?"

He was grateful when his first participation in combat found him able to perform his job and conduct himself bravely. With a sincerity and faith that the self-exiled American expatriates would later find an illusion, he wrote, thinking of himself as well:

"American manhood is bound to be better for this experience. Previous to this so many thousands of us had no particular purpose in living, only to plod and work. This has broadened us and given us a purpose in life."

He was the small town boy in a letter to his father in early November of 1918:

"What would you have said three years ago

if someone told you I would some day be peering through a 30-power glass and look right into the German front line trenches on the western front. And see as far as ten miles in the rear of his lines. Would you believe it? Neither would I. I could see the Boche but he couldn't see me. Maybe it was just as well for he is particular about people peeking at what he is doing."

The discomfort and tediousness of the hours between battle wore on him, and in a note at this time, he begins to sound more like a front line soldier of any war in any place.

"It is now Tuesday eve. All day today it rained steady as well as yesterday and the day before. I don't see where and why all the rain in this country and yet they are always still short of water."

On Sunday evening, the tenth of November, 1918, with all the front waiting for news of the German surrender, he wrote with the bountiful enthusiasm of a young boy:

"Isn't today a big day? Aren't all of these last few days big days? Whether she surrenders today or tomorrow she is finished and her days are numbered. By the time you receive this I may be living in a castle on the Rhine—reorganizing the Rhine wine industry. Boy, won't that be great?"

And when the news was definite, he wrote again in a letter dated November twelfth:

"All day yesterday the bells of the neighboring churches pealed ceaselessly. The demonstration in Paris was gigantic. The people went wild. All France is gleaming with joy.''

A period of waiting set in. The endless and eternal waiting of soldiers to be shipped home after the completion of a war. Galvin waited, impatient as the rest, the tenor of the days taking on a certain monotony.

Burley had been attending De Paul University in Chicago and when the war finished he packed up to return home to Harvard. Galvin in his new awareness of the world outside the borders of Harvard berated them all:

''I received Burley's letter this A.M. and it disappointed me very much. I say to him get out —if you have to drive a coal wagon somewhere— but he will never get anywhere in a thousand years in a small town with only a one-horse factory and a bunch of knockers. Oh, I know how you all get together at home and figure, figure, figure —Hell—figuring doesn't get anyone anywhere but doing will.''

But a few days later, in a more temperate vein, he could write:

''Dear folks: I was glad to receive your letter with the precise reason Burley did not continue with De Paul. I feel a bit better about it now than when I wrote that letter.''

Later, in the same letter, he wrote impatiently:

''We are still waiting and expect to wait a

few more weeks. Each week will help a bit to allow the storm season to pass before we sail. But I would take on a storm just to get home sooner.''

Galvin was discharged from Camp Bowie, Texas in the early spring of 1919. He had cabled his family when he expected to arrive in Harvard, but the wire had gone astray. He caught them all by surprise on the day of his return. He found his father and brothers in a store near the station, and in a triumphant group accompanied by a number of jubilant townspeople, they marched back to the house to his mother and sister.

Word was carried to his grandfather and grandmother Brickley on the outskirts of town. The afternoon turned bad and by nightfall a severe storm shook the area. Grandfather Brickley had been ill and his wife and daughter would not let him go with them to the Galvin house, promising him that Paul would come and see him the next day. But the old man would not be denied the first night of his grandson's triumphant return from the war. As they left by the front door, he slipped out the back and hurried through the storm to arrive at the Galvin house moments after his wife and daughter arrived. It was a festive night that the members of the family would remember all the rest of their lives.

It was indeed an exultant time, a rejoicing for Americans similar to that which possessed Athenians after the defeat of the Persians at Marathon, and, by Englishmen, after the defeat of the mighty Spanish Armada. Life seen through victory flashed a prism of bright and vigorous colors.

It was also a tragic time. The cost of the war in human terms had been dreadful.

Ahead were the meetings in the palace of Versailles, the long and bitter debates, and a sick and exhausted President Wilson seeking to rally men to his vision. With his defeat the dead of the Marne, Belleau Wood, the Argonne Forest would seem to have died in vain. Forced to abandon grace in the face of victory, the country would hurtle into prohibition, crime, and violence.

Another more brittle and sophisticated segment of Galvin's generation would be repelled and disillusioned by the war and the loss of the peace. The American expatriates would flee to Paris and gaze with angry and lonely eyes at the land they felt had abandoned them. Scott Fitzgerald would live and write the frenetic escapades and furious pleasures of the Jazz Age, and of "young people who wore out early—who became hard and languid at twenty-one—bloated, glutted, stupid with cakes and circuses."

But along with many other young men who had no Fitzgerald to chronicle them, Galvin had found in the war a strengthening of his faith in himself and in his land. He would never forget the lessons of his army experience, the welding together of men into a company which would not disintegrate in a situation of crisis. There was above all else a loyalty to one's own. A good soldier stands by his comrades, a good officer looks after his men.

The important thing was that he felt toughened, more confident of what he might have to face, because of his experience in the war. For this reason he was spared the murderous self-pity which came with boredom and indolence. He knew that he had come a long way from the early days in Harvard, from the popcorn baskets and the ice cream cones. He had been across the ocean and had commanded men in battle. For the gilded moment he was full of hope and courage.

Batteries
and Bust
5

By the end of the First World War, a series of momentous developments were taking place across the country. Electric power was displacing the steam engine. Airplanes, greatly improved through the war, would soon fly passengers.

For energy, gasoline and fuel oil were gaining rapidly on coal. Modern machinery, made of alloyed metals, was changing the appearance and altering the tempo of factories. Electrically powered assembly lines were introducing a new phase to the Industrial Revolution.

A new American society was forming, and creating an economy to sustain it far removed from the economy of the farm. Most important of all, the automobile industry was developing with startling rapidity, pressing the rapid development of products made of glass, rubber, and steel.

The 1920s established the "car" as a basic necessity. It became a symbol of prestige and affluence. The nation rode on wheels with mounting excitement, felt in this increased pace a movement toward a more majestic destiny.

The reverberations of these massive changes swept across the nation, and the winds of growth and change were felt even in the small towns. In Harvard, Galvin heard them, and felt them, finding a resounding answer in his own heart. He realized that these advances in science and technology would affect business and economic change. He had heard and read of the great new oil fields in Texas and for a while envisaged making his for-

tune in them quickly. He corresponded with
some of the oil people, his letters shamelessly im-
modest but sincere in stating his qualifications,
and on the strength of his enthusiasm and his experience he was promised a job in July in Waco,
Texas. But that still left sixty days from the time
of his discharge and in his mood of excitement and
jubilation that seemed an eternity. When he was
offered a job for the D & G Storage Battery Company in Chicago, which made electric storage
batteries for use in automobiles, he took it as a
temporary measure in order to make every day
count.

"I don't know what would have happened if I
had waited on that Waco job," he recalled later.
"I might have gone down there and worked as a
rigger-helper and really gotten hold of the oil
thing, or I might have just stayed a rigger-helper
for twenty years."

In Chicago, he roomed again with his aunt
Helen and uncle Jack Kehoe. And the aura of anticipation which mantled his return from overseas
was dispelled in the long, relentless days at the
storage battery company. He found little time in
which to correspond home, and his letters in this
period were brief and fragmentary. He managed
to visit Harvard at least once a week and for a
day the family was reunited, and he and Lillian
made plans for their marriage.

Galvin worked for the storage battery company all through 1920, pausing only briefly on the

twenty-fourth of April to marry Lillian at St. Joseph's Church in Harvard and set up housekeeping with her in Chicago. They had had a long and amiable relationship, knew each other well and thought themselves sensibly oriented to the demands of marriage upon each other. She understood his ambition, his dream to make a place for himself in business, and she wanted to help him achieve it.

Toward the end of 1920, Philip Galvin's health grew worse and a certain desperate tone entered Galvin's letters to his brother, encouraging him, admonishing him to take care of himself, letting him share in the details of the business as if hoping in myriad small ways to give him these additional links to life. In Galvin's letters great stress was laid on "ordinary common sense." He had, even at this early age, a capacity of foreseeing horizons broader than those visible to most people. Mostly he had a strange, sometimes obsessive, feeling that work was sacred; that it could accomplish miracles. He would have thoroughly affirmed the truth of Allan Nevin's quoting Henry Ford as saying, "Work does more than get us our living; it gets us our life."

The boom touched off by the war and sustained by spending for reconstruction broke in the middle of 1920. The resulting effect was major in the sudden decline on volume of business and small businessmen unable to sustain the sharp recurring valleys and peaks were buffeted relent-

lessly. There were small periodic improvements
lasting a month or two, followed by equally sudden declines.

The year 1920 marked a substantial move
forward in the field of radio. There was practically no home radio of significance across the
country and the air was inhabited by wireless
amateurs or "hams" who sat up nights exchang-
ing code with one another or listening to the mes-
sages from ships at sea. KDKA Pittsburgh began
broadcasting on November 22, 1920. This opening
came about through a research broadcast station
in a barn set up by Dr. Frank Conrad of Westing-
house Electric. Though at first used only for music
and baseball scores, the great potential of this
new medium was soon grasped. The first public
service broadcast was station KDKA's reporting
of the Harding-Cox election returns.

Some of the early broadcasts were abomina-
ble, but the innovation of this kind of entertain-
ment carried its own excitement. The forerunner
of the late television movie was established by
listeners remaining up through the night listening
to the early radio broadcasts. More and more
people bought radio equipment. Stations began
coming on the air around the country, each gener-
ating a ring of radio receivers around it. The
growth of both radio and the automobile provided
the incentive and opportunity for Galvin's next
move.

Edward Stewart was an energetic and tempestuous man born in Big Foot, Illinois, who had known Galvin in Harvard and could match him ambition for ambition. He had been active in radio for some years as head of the Stewart Acme Reflex Radio.

In early 1921, Stewart approached Galvin on the possibility of their entering business together. They were both young, energetic and enterprising men with an adroit capacity to balance their dreams on the wheels of hard labor. Stewart had the capacity to sell his ideas to others, and, with an evangelist's zeal, he parlayed these ideas. The Chamber of Commerce of Marshfield, Wisconsin wanted a manufacturing plant. Stewart spoke to Galvin about a storage battery plant and the cooperation the town would provide.

Eager to get out on his own, Galvin agreed. In early July of 1921, at the age of twenty-six, he and Lillian prepared to move from Chicago to Marshfield.

With great fanfare the Stewart Battery Company was opened in Marshfield on July 15, 1921. The Chamber of Commerce congratulated Stewart and Galvin and themselves in this sagacious joining of talents.

The company was a consolidation of two battery plants, the Stewart-Galvin Battery Company, and the Stewart-Storage Battery Company. Stewart-Galvin was the manufacturing part of the partnership, while the Stewart Storage Battery Company was the distribution and selling

agent. The company occupied the main floor and
office space of what had been the Marshfield-
Franklin garage. They offered employment to approximately fifty people.

When a reporter from the Marshfield paper
approached Galvin for an answer as to why they
had located in Marshfield, he stated firmly that the
city was ideally situated. Railroad connections
were excellent and the city was located in a prosperous and progressive ring of small towns.

The first months of operation did nothing to
dampen the surge of enthusiasm which everybody
felt. And the paper could go on to report that
Stewart-Galvin was "one of the largest of Marshfield's manufacturing industries producing approximately 150 storage batteries a day, with a
distribution covering Wisconsin, Iowa, Min-
nesota, Illinois, Nebraska, Kansas, Oklahoma,
Arkansas, Mississippi, Tennessee and Kentucky,
and reaching as far east as Massachusetts. It has
a branch distributing house located in Kansas
City."

With recollections of their popcorn success
as a team, Joseph Galvin came from Harvard to
work in the Marshfield plant and added his effort
to that of his brother. On August 14th, Galvin
wrote to Phil:

"I have been buried and I am just now getting my head above water. It has been a tough pull
night and day. Six in the morning to 11 p.m. for

the last two weeks including Sunday. I barely get any time to spend with Lillian.

"Our first forming came off today, and thanks to all it was a dandy. We will start shipping batteries by Tuesday and then we will be on our way.

"Joe has been on the job right with me, a big help and he is also dog tired every night. There's no news outside of the shop excepting we are still boarding and rooming, and no sight of a house. Some sport for Lillian.

"Stick with it, old boy. Keep resting and fighting and thinking that you are going to lick this thing. Your wonderful spirit aids in spurring me on when I feel down sometimes, and I do thank you deeply for that. You are going to win, Phil."

In that same month, Joe Galvin wrote to Phil as well with news of how he was spending his time:

"It is quite a sacrifice to come up here and work for the wages I am getting and considering the work that I am doing. But it's just like the army, learn as you earn, and by working very hard I am making a better and quicker chance for my promotion. I am working every night that Paul does. You know our brother and you know how much work that means."

While the brothers struggled in Marshfield to keep the battery company alive, Phil back in Harvard grew steadily worse. In September of 1921, he suffered a setback, and Galvin's letters to him became almost frantic in an effort to provide his dying brother with the energy and determination that might help him overcome his ailment.

"I am taking a great lesson from you; a lesson of courage and of patience," Galvin wrote. "Do not give up, do not give up! If you could have read my heart several times even in these past few months, you would have seen that many times I did want to give up and thought all our work was useless and it was impossible for us to survive. But I stick it out and keep hoping and keep fighting. And in this battle your wonderful courage helps sustain me and I want you to know that you have helped me more than I could ever help you."

In another letter, a few days later to Phil, one of the last before his brother's death, he cried:

"Spirit! spirit! spirit! The decider of all perplexities. Without it we are lost."

The death of Philip Galvin on September 29, 1921, was expected and feared and yet was a great blow to the entire family. Galvin's relationship to Phil had been almost that of a father rather than that of an older brother. In many ways he saw the younger boy possessed of qualities which he felt he did not have; a certain burning grace and innocence, a loveliness of spirit. All the rest of his life he would never forget Phil and would retain his brother's letters as something to be treasured

and reread at regular intervals. He took what
consolation he could in his faith and drove himself harder at work. On October 10, 1921, he wrote
to his mother:

"We all have our moments when we remember Phil, and I guess it will be that way for as
long as we live. I find myself suddenly stopping
whatever I am doing and thinking that he can not
really be gone. There is nothing to do then but
keep working and try to remember all the good
moments we had together."

A few weeks later, he wrote to his father:

"Business is an intricate thing, and especially now in these days of tight money. But ham-
mering and digging and scrapping will beat it and
some day (I hope) we will be representative of a
big successful concern.

"This I know you hope for even more than
we do. Joe is back on the job today, which was a
grand relief to me. Next week I am going to turn
over the Assembly Department to him. And it is
on his merits too—not because he is my brother.
He earns his own way, which I know is most
gratifying to you."

But all their effort was doomed to failure as
the country began to feel the effects of the 1920–
21 depression, and they found out the location had
many disadvantages. Marshfield was a full day
away from Chicago—the central shipping point to
other parts of the country.

"We discovered we had the poorest place in
the world for a storage battery operation," Galvin said wryly years later, "because batteries involved so much weight. We were closed off from
the bigger markets by the economics of shipping.
The storage batteries were heavy, messy to ship
and the acid in them made the rate classification
high. The manufacturer that was located in the
bigger markets had the edge on us. Why didn't we
think of all this at the beginning? Hell, I don't
know."

They managed to hang on through 1922. And
on October ninth, their first and only child, Robert
William, was born at St. Joseph's Hospital in
Marshfield. Galvin was jubilant about the birth of
his son.

With a stubborn refusal to acknowledge the
handwriting on the wall, Stewart and Galvin
fought on through the early months of 1923. The
end came swiftly and suddenly while Galvin was
at home for lunch one day when government
agents moved in and padlocked the plant for non-
payment of excise tax on storage batteries. When
Galvin returned from lunch, he could not re-enter
the shop to retrieve his overcoat, the only one he
had.

"I kept thinking about that coat. Having the
business closed down was bad news, but somehow
losing that coat bothered me just as much. I kept
thinking that the government had a right to close

the business but didn't have a right to take my coat.''

During the next sixty days Galvin and Stewart did everything they could to save the business, but it was a lost cause. They tried energetically and unsuccessfully to float a loan. They had several additional meetings with the Chamber of Commerce, but the general economic condition of the country was against them. The *Marshfield Herald* on August 2, 1923, wrote the obituary:

''Monday afternoon the office equipment and factory supplies of the defunct Stewart-Galvin Battery Company were placed on sale by the government officials to secure payment of unpaid taxes.''

A few days later, with only a dollar and a half in his pocket, Galvin packed his wife, Lillian, and their ten-month-old son, Bob, into a broken down old car and started back to Illinois. This wasn't enough money for their meals except that he arranged to carry one of the company's employees who also wanted to get back to Chicago. The rider's share of the expenses for the trip would provide the Galvin family with money to eat during the journey. They started from Marshfield on August 2, 1923, the day the country was shocked by news of President Harding's death. ''It felt like the whole world was dropping out from under us,'' Galvin said.

The item in the Marshfield Herald covering

their departure was considerably more brief and
less enthusiastic than the one which had heralded
their arrival:

"Mr. and Mrs. P. V. Galvin, after a few
years' residence in this city, moved last week to
their former home in Chicago."

Eliminators
and Trust
6

Once again Galvin returned briefly to Harvard. This time not as an exuberant war hero, but as a man who had so much faith in hard work that when it did not suffice, he was stung by frustration and fury. He could not visualize himself remaining in Harvard, settling for the less stringent requirements of the small town, and for this reason he was restless to leave. A return to any business of his own at this time was out of the question. He borrowed $30 or $40 from his father, and on the strength of a job offer from Emil Brach, who had married his aunt Kate Cunningham, he started again for Chicago.

The young Galvins found a place to rent on West End Avenue in Chicago, a far cry from the open spaces and quiet of Marshfield and Harvard.

The job with Emil Brach lasted three years from 1923 into 1926. Brach was in his sixties at that time, still vigorously leading almost every phase of his company's operation. He had started the Brach Candy Company as a young man and built it into a position of national prominence. For Galvin the three years were time to regroup his forces and gain additional experience. He worked as personal secretary to Brach and was an avid student of each phase of the company's business. Some of the older man's iron firmness and vigor impressed itself upon Galvin. He was able in this time to recognize the insufficiency of hard work alone, unless it were tempered and guided by direction and good sense. When problems developed in the shop, he participated in their evaluation and solution and made it his business to anticipate bottlenecks.

"He was kind of a snoopy fellow," an old Brach employee of that time recalls, "concerned with everything that went on. If we had a problem, he wasn't content to know that it was solved but wanted to know how."

In 1926 Brach retired to move to California. Galvin was offered a position with the company in sales, and he considered the offer seriously because he respected the company and liked the associations. But he did not think of himself primarily as a salesman, and his vision of being in business for himself remained strong. With calculated irony, fate brought him back into contact with Ed Stewart from Marshfield. Stewart, through his father, had bought up the remains of the battery company in Marshfield at the time of the government foreclosure and had moved it to a Peoria Street location in Chicago that seemed to answer the original problem of location. They seemed to be well set to take advantage of an expanding market. The two men met to talk of a second association and struck sparks from the flint of one another's enthusiasm.

On the surface of things 1926 was a good time for the manufacturing business. The economic vacillations of the early twenties had settled into a steady ascent. Research and technology had

Grandfather and
Grandmother Brickley

Grandmother Galvin.
No picture remains
of Grandfather Galvin

Alice Brickley Galvin
and John Charles Galvin
on their wedding day,
January 31, 1894

Paul Vincent Galvin

Paul, Joe, and Raymond (Burley)

Dad and three boys, Joe, Paul, and Raymond

opened up new areas for exploration and development. The war seemed far away and the caution of the years immediately following were austere and unfashionable. New conveniences were available and people wished to avail themselves of the comforts they offered.

Automobiles were getting bigger and better every month, outdistancing the development of roads. Five years before, in 1921, there had not been a single numbered highway in America. Recommended equipment for travel outside the city limits was "chains on all four wheels and a shovel with a collapsible handle." But the situation had changed rapidly and good roads were spreading out in all directions.

Even in a booming 1926 economy the radio was exceptional.

In 1920, when Galvin moved to Marshfield, there were an estimated 3,000 radios scattered across the country. Just two years later there were almost 300,000 sets. By 1926 radio sales had already gone beyond a half billion dollar annual volume.

Although the Stewart battery business appeared to be thriving, both the men knew that the development of alternating current radio was just a matter of time. Because batteries were bulky, messy and had to be replaced in the space of a couple of years, the battery set would be a thing of the past. In the meantime, there were more than five million battery sets in use across the

country, and five million people had invested
money in them. Most of these sets were no more
than a year or two old. People wanted the con-
venience of AC but had a natural objection
against throwing away their battery sets. Stewart
suggested meeting the most difficult part of this
problem with a simple little device called the A-
Eliminator. This unit consisted of a small trickle
charger that worked together with the "A" or
storage battery in one package. The unit was
plugged into an electric outlet and the radio into
the Eliminator. The radio drew filament power it
needed from the "A" battery and the trickle
charger kept the battery charged.

Galvin bought in for a small share of the
business, and this money was used to purchase
components, the assembly line set up and the
eliminators launched into production. The hand-
bills and circulars which they had printed and cir-
culated in that period cried the merits of their
products and guaranteed each phase of the operation.

"We were running a good house," Galvin
said. "We were making a good storage battery
and had some nice accounts. We were even doing
carload business and the A-Eliminator had real
potential. It worked just fine—in the shop."

For a while, Galvin and Stewart rode the
crest of prosperity, and then a few reports came
back to them from the field of defective units. The
rectifier that was used in the A-Eliminator turned

out balky under actual field conditions. More and more of the units began coming back and soon Stewart and Galvin were again caught in an uncomfortably familiar position. They called back the units they had shipped and began a twenty-four hour day engineering crash program to iron out the kinks. Given time, the problem might have been solved, but in 1928 everything was available except time.

Competition was fierce and if a company's products did not work, the customers quickly went elsewhere. Stewart and Galvin fought for time and were joined in their efforts by a brilliant young engineer named Dwight Eddleman who began working on a dry eliminator that eliminated the storage battery and used a different kind of rectifier. The question became whether they could develop this dry eliminator before going under. Stewart negotiated the possibility of taking in an additional partner who would provide sorely needed funds, but these talks fell through because they did not wish to relinquish control. Another method they used to relieve the constantly increasing pressure was to sell their accounts receivable, selling them generally at 70 per cent of the invoice figure and being charged a substantial rate of interest on the total invoice amount.

"We tried to buy time," Galvin recalled. "We got an appointment with General Wood at Sears Roebuck and demonstrated this dry A-

Eliminator. There wasn't anything like it on the
market. It wasn't quite ready for marketing yet,
but we hoped we would have it ready in a few
months. They sent some samples to their laboratories which returned impressive reports.''

On the strength of the prospective eliminator
and the possibility of another partner who would
bring funds into the company, Stewart and Galvin
had been able to keep their creditors at bay. As
soon as word got out that the negotiations with
the financial interest had collapsed, the creditors
hit in a storm and the sheriff closed the business
down. The storage battery end of the business was
bought by another company; and the eliminator
end, together with a few tools and machines, went
on auction.

''About the time we closed that business I got
a call from the head of the radio department at
Sears,'' Galvin said, ''suggesting I pick up the
Stewart eliminators and start a little business of
my own. They would catalogue them and buy
enough to make it worthwhile. They encouraged
me into thinking about buying up that end of the
business that was up for auction.''

To reassure himself that he would not be dependent upon Sears alone, Galvin and his brother
Joe, who had again joined him in 1926, canvassed
South State Street calling on the managers of as
many radio stores as they could find. After a
couple of days of concerted effort they had a dozen

more outlets lined up who would buy the eliminator at a reasonable price.

On the day of the auction Galvin had managed to raise approximately $1,000, but if the bidding for the eliminator exceeded that amount he was through. He brought along Joe and young Les Harder, who worked in the stockroom of the battery company, to point out the needed components so that Galvin would not bid on anything that wasn't absolutely essential. With all of this caution there was still a question whether a shop to manufacture the eliminator could be formed, a location found, and the final kinks ironed out. In the absence of anything more substantial the eliminator at least offered a tenuous prospect.

The property was sold in batches of office furniture, fixtures and tools. Galvin listened carefully for clues as to who might bid against him for the eliminator. The final item for sale was the complete tools, plans and designs, working models and good will for the manufacture and sale of the Battery Eliminator.

There were several opening bids of a few hundred dollars and the bidding moved desultorily along until it reached the five hundred dollar mark. It was a moment Galvin would never forget.

"I wanted that eliminator so much," he recalled later. "Any prospect of continuing in business on my own dangled by a thread so slim a couple of hundred dollars could cut it."

The bidding for the eliminator had been jumping by fifty and a hundred dollars at a time, and Galvin decided upon a bold although precarious show of confidence and power by jumping two hundred and fifty dollars and holding the final two hundred and fifty in reserve for a last, and for him, final move. The jump of two hundred and fifty dollars in the bidding scared off the competitive bidders who had little faith in the product anyway, and that portion of the business was sold to Galvin for a little over seven hundred and fifty dollars.

In later years, a legend developed around a figure of $565 with which "Paul Galvin started Motorola." In reality this $565 figure represented his working capital when he began operations and did not include the $750 which he paid at the auction for the tools, plans and design of the battery eliminator. Considering the remarkable growth of the company, any question about a few hundred dollars at its inception would hardly seem to dim the brightness of the achievement.

"That's how I got into the eliminator business," Galvin said. "Although even then I knew I wasn't going to be there very long, because the time wasn't far off when people were going to be buying only new sets with AC tubes."

Shortly after the auction, Joe Galvin began to call the men who had worked with him in the shop asking them to come down and talk to him on a matter of importance.

"There's Paul an' there's me," he said seriously to each man, "and if you work like hell there's you in the number three slot. We are giving you a chance to get in on the ground floor of what is going to be a great company and grow with it."

Joe was well liked and his fierce loyalty toward his people was well known. He was a generous friend even though in the shop he was regarded as a stern taskmaster. Although Galvin was not quite as close to many of the men and perhaps a little more reserved than Joe, he was respected by those who worked with him. These personal factors were almost enough to bring men in determined to work hard for the small new company, and Joe's canny emphasis upon the lineup stressing the benefits of hard work was an added inducement.

In actual practice in the years to come as business improved and the company grew, most of these early employees would be rewarded beyond any expectation they or the Galvins might have anticipated.

The Uncertain Birth
7

The Galvin Manufacturing Corporation was born on September 25, 1928, in a small section of a rented building at 847 Harrison Street in Chicago with five employees.

The Harrison Street building was a six story brick structure with a watertower on the roof. The location was a neighborhood of warehouses and small factories and the food shops of Greek and Italian immigrants. The streets rang with the cry of apple vendors. Galvin made arrangements to take over half of the first floor—the other tenant on the floor was the Midwest Slipper Company—and there was some storage space in the basement. Most of the floors above them were empty or only partly occupied by seasonal businesses. Perhaps this grim rental situation assisted Galvin in his early agreement with the landlord, who wanted him to sign a lease for a year.

"You know how much money I have," Galvin told the landlord. "Signing a lease doesn't mean anything because that is all there is. And this is a good time for me to tell you that I can't pay the first month's rent until the end of the month. I know it's customary to pay in advance but I'm working so close I just won't have the money for a few weeks."

The Harrison Street operation in those first months was precarious with nothing being bought that couldn't be instantly used. The first week's payroll was $63.

For a while they existed tenuously on the re-

pair of eliminators which Sears Roebuck had
sold through their catalogue and had returned for
service during the warranty period. All of Galvin's slim working capital went for components to
replace defective parts. When he and Joe could
make some arrangement for marginal credit, they
purchased a few extra parts and began to manufacture some new A and B Eliminators which they
sold to any outlet that would purchase them.

There is an art in business as there is in anything else, an art of anticipation and an acumen
that comes out of experience plus a certain sensitivity. Galvin had this art. He knew that the
eliminator was not going to provide them a market for very long. Even then AC radio was beginning to come into use, with countless loft operators producing a variety of sets. Dominating the
field was the competition of such strong producers
as Atwater-Kent, Kennedy, Sparton, Majestic,
Zenith, RCA and GE.

Galvin made a precarious invasion of the
home radio field, and began to manufacture some
AC sets, basically a nine-tube chassis with as-
sorted name plates for private-label sale. They
would manufacture a standard set and then have a
certain name plate to put on it out of a selection
of about twenty suppliers' names.

This early manufacturing was a haphazard
operation, because their lack of working capital
did not allow the purchase of tools and dies. They
had to go to a sheet metal concern and have chassis

blanks cut to size. They would finish the operation
themselves by drilling the blanks to fit the parts.
Everybody would be pressed into some phase of
the operation, and to Joe and a few others fell the
task of drilling these blanks. In the beginning,
being more willing than competent, they would
break or wear out a series of drills. For a while
the constant purchasing of drills to replace the
broken ones added another burden on their precarious finances.

The wild fluctuations of that early market required an extremely flexible production. When
sets were ordered, they had to be produced
quickly and delivered immediately. If an order
was not filled rapidly enough one of the numerous
competitors could easily slip into the breach. The
problem became one of having to produce a batch
of sets almost overnight.

When Galvin brought in a rush order, Joe
would commandeer additional space in the building on one of the empty floors and overnight would
run wiring up through the walls to these floors and
set up work benches and tables. In the morning,
they drew additional manpower for these tables
from the line of people that waited each day for
work outside of the building. Their own men under
the stern direction of Joe supervised the production.

In this manner of movement, they might have
provided material for a ''Keystone Kop'' comedy
as they juggled their benches all over the building.

Some space vacant the night before would be operating busily with men and tables in the morning, and the following night would have benches and wires dismantled and removed again.

The distraught landlord sought to keep them contained within their rented premises and threatened legal action against them. But because of the necessity of survival the forays into other parts of the building continued.

"It was the damndest thing," an old employee of that time recalls. "Those tables and that wiring used to appear and disappear like magic. I remember once, when there was no space available anywhere else, Joe set up a couple of boys on a table in the men's washroom."

At this stage the company's bookkeeping was almost as basic as it had been for the popcorn business back in Harvard. The whole question of paydays became a matter of massive concern for everyone. Early in the afternoon of payday one of the men, often Joe, would load up a few eliminators and some radio chassis and take them down to be sold to some of the radio outlet shops on South State Street. Then he would hurry back with the cash in order to meet the payroll.

Sometimes, the sets that were delivered to customers required instant collection of the cash and Earl McGowan, who had worked with Galvin from the days of Stewart Battery, became a specialist at this tenuous but essential kind of collecting.

"I took out about fifteen or eighteen chassis with strict orders from Joe to get the cash for them. We needed it or no one would get paid that day. The fellow I delivered the sets to gave me a check and looked uneasily at the bank across the street on which the check had been drawn. He was stalling around till closing time. I had been through this before and knew a way of getting down to the vault and then back upstairs to the bank in time to get the check certified. He stalled me off until he saw the guard close the bank's front door.

"I took the check and ran downstairs through the vault and then up to the bank where I pleaded with the teller to help me out. Sure enough—insufficient funds. I started back to the customer and he must have seen me coming because he proceeded to beat it. On a hunch I headed for the freight elevator and met him there. 'I can't accept your check, sir,' I said politely. 'I got to have the cash.' So he went back upstairs and dug around and borrowed some from a fellow next door and I got the cash."

Galvin knew that manufacturing unbranded sets left them at the mercy of the buyer. "They knew how much it cost us to produce a set," he said. "We weren't able—nor did we expect—to make any sizeable profit on our product. Just around the corner a few other fellows were manufacturing in another loft. This pattern was being repeated in a hundred lofts all over the city. We were making fifty cents a set on our radios and averaging about 100 sets a day. There were a lot of days when we didn't make that, of course, and I knew the day would come when these unbranded sets would be outmoded too. But meanwhile they kept us alive.''

Galvin had worked long and hard and had known desperation before. But the operation in those early months of the new business required the most strenuous effort he and Joe had ever been called upon to make. Because of their narrow margin of profit they could not allow any aspect of the operation to go uncontrolled. Although Galvin was not an engineer, he sensed when there was some particular shop problem. A man working late at his bench would not be surprised to see Galvin at his elbow and hear him ask, ''How's it going?''

They were perpetually surprised at how much he knew of what was going on. They understood how Joe, who worked beside them in the shop, might be able to keep tab, but Galvin was out on the street a good deal of the time contacting accounts and suppliers.

In his relationship with his employees, he was recognized as tough but also very fair. He knew the complexity of their problems and was tolerant of a man trying to unravel one of these problems, but he would become infuriated by signs of bungling. If he felt the men needed prodding, he would read them the riot act at a meeting called

on the spur of the moment. This was a harbinger
of the days some years later when in their Augusta plant he would stick his head out of his
office along Mahogany Row and summarily sum-
mon his vice-presidents to a "board-meeting" at
which he grimly promised, "some noses are going
to get pushed back."

                    *   *   *   *

    For the most part the men who worked in the
Galvin shop in those early days were men without
formal engineering degrees, but men who loved
radio and had tinkered with it from the time they
were boys.

    An engineer at this time who did some bold
designing for Galvin was Bill Lear, who occupied
space in the Harrison Street building for his own
firm, Radio Coil and Wire. He was a brilliant and
unpredictably buoyant man who had a productive
though sometimes erratic association with Galvin
for a number of years.

    Bill Lear designed his own coils for radios.
The most efficient wire used for RF coils up to
that time was Litz wire, expensively imported
from Germany. This consisted of 5 to 11 strands
of fine wire, each separately insulated from the
others, and then wound together. Bill Lear made
his own Litz wire and arranged that this wire be
used as a component in any of the sets he designed.

    Lear was also responsible for bringing into
the Galvin employ a bright radio man named

Elmer Wavering, who some thirty-two years later would become president of Motorola. As a boy in his home town of Quincy, Illinois, Wavering had been vitally interested in radio and had taught himself to assemble and disassemble a number of radio sets. His first contact with Lear, who was also from Quincy, came when he saw a sign in the window of Lear's small radio shop advertising for a radio technician. Wavering rushed home to put on his best suit and hurried back to earnestly and successfully convince Lear that he fitted the bill.

Later on, Wavering opened a small radio service business of his own in Quincy until, through Lear, he met Galvin and did several free-lance assignments for him over a period of time. Finally he began the permanent association with Galvin that was to grow always closer in the following thirty years.

Galvin would storm at him in outbursts of temper when Wavering stood obstinately for some course he felt strongly was right. But their great affection for each other thrived and Galvin, always appreciative of loyalty, often conceded his debt to Wavering. More perhaps than any other man in the company besides Joe, Elmer Wavering suffered and shared the disappointments and struggles of those merciless early years.

It was true that most of the men who worked at Harrison Street in those first years were robust dissenters. They disagreed with each other as vigorously as they fought their competition, and

yet for all the hard work, they managed to laugh
and find numerous ways to dramatize their plight.
Since desks were at a premium, Al Ocken, a key
mechanical engineer, had a memo pad titled,
"from the packing case of Al Ocken." Don
Mitchell, who later would become chief engineer
for Galvin, had in those pioneer days a legendary
"simple bending tool" which could apparently
perform prodigious feats. Whether the problem
consisted of a plumbing impediment in the washroom or some involved aspect of a radio chassis,
Mitchell's "simple bending tool" was invariably
called upon to meet the emergency.

Another source of laughter and agitation was
the building elevator, an erratic and uncertain
monster, operated with great dignity by "Dad"
Coon. On numerous occasions it became jammed
between floors and the ropes had to be pulled
manually in order to get it moving again. A sharp
call for "Dad" Coon would find a delayed response, because, like one of the somber proverbial
Volga boatmen, he grimly and slowly would be
hauling himself up the shaft.

"In addition we were always afraid the elevator was going to fall," someone said, "but
'Dad' Coon calmed us down and eventually got us
to the floor we wanted."

After a while, because of the delays, it became an unwritten law that the elevator be used
for freight only. While this constituted no hardship when Galvin Manufacturing occupied only

the first two floors and had less than a hundred people, the same could not be said for the company operations when it expanded to include the entire six floors, and had eight hundred employees.

Another early but elderly employee was Hugo Kraenzle, who staked his claim in the company on a hand cart with a sign reading "this truck belongs to Hugo." Galvin—always loyal to those who were loyal to him—was almost superstitious about Hugo. Once when some foreman fired Hugo in Galvin's absence, Galvin returned and rehired him at once. He said of Hugo, "if this company ever goes under, the last two guys out the door will be Hugo and me."

In those days, on Chicago's west side, as well as throughout most of the country during the 1920s, drinking was an institution attended to with grave dignity and dedication. Prohibition had driven the corner saloons behind locked doors and had given them, in the process, an aura of romance and danger. Men finishing long and hard weeks in factories and offices needed release and nothing was calculated to achieve this release more explosively than in some monumental drinking bouts on bootlegger's booze. Expected back to work on Monday morning a man who had begun hitting the "speakeasys" on Friday evening might not return to his job until Wednesday. This played havoc with the schedules and became a serious problem.

Galvin's robust and hard-working employees were no exception to this rule. To meet the situation and the acute problem of absenteeism it occasionally produced, Galvin devised a plan. The more sober of the employees were assigned to accompany the violent drinkers on their rounds on Friday and Saturday night and make sure they could report for work on Monday. So fiercely did Galvin make these pursuers feel their responsibility that one followed his man from speakeasy to speakeasy and when he saw him collapse in an alley from which he could not be raised "got right down and sat beside him so I'd be sure to be there when he woke up."

Although he would later cease drinking and smoking completely, at this time Galvin did occasionally enjoy a drink and a cigar. Sympathetic, because he shared the pressures under which his men worked, he could be indulgent about their celebrations and not object to a man "enjoying himself as he pleased." But when this celebrating rendered a man unable to perform his work properly, or get to his work at all, then Galvin saw it as "a damn fool thing." He always remained sensitive to the dimensions of the problem, and shortly after prohibition had been repealed, when a Christmas party in the shop became a near-riot, he ordered all liquor off the premises for good.

By 1929, radio was an 840 million dollar annual business, up 1,400 per cent in just seven years. The screen grid tube had made it possible to give sets much greater sensitivity with fewer tubes. All new home radios were now AC operated. By the summer of 1929, the stock market had risen fantastically and the radio stocks were some of the leaders in the rise.

Aided by the frenzied demands of an economy caught in the throes of an irresponsible ascent orders for Galvin's home radios continued to increase. Every week more employees joined the company and the operation extended to other floors. It was Joe's responsibility to fit these new people in and get them set up for work. On many nights, the light burned in his small front office well past midnight as he sought to prepare for work the next day.

Many manufacturers, ignoring the discernible omens of catastrophe, geared their plants for a tremendous year. Dealers loaded their stores with merchandise for fall and amply secured their inventories for what everyone felt would be a record-breaking holiday season. Consumers, joyous at the bountiful stock market profits which seemed endless, searched zestfully for products on which to spend their papier-mâché wealth.

The Bull Market of 1927–29 was propped up by the investments of people bidding up the price of stocks without analyzing the earnings record of the companies involved. Fanciful prospectuses created euphoric vistas for the companies.

And then on "Black Friday," October 25,

1929, the stock market, like a bewildered bull, suddenly caught by the charge of a hundred matadors, twisted and shuddered and fell.

Almost overnight the whole business climate changed. Marketing became a vast, hysterical game of "hot potato" with everyone trying to reduce their inventories and get rid of their merchandise.

In some of the earlier disruptions of the market, Galvin had remained unaffected. Working on a few eliminators returned under warranty and making a handful of AC sets, he could sit out the storm. But after the crash of 1929, with a considerable inventory and an energetic and productive shop, he was staggered when the big manufacturers dumped their brand name sets upon the market at prices well under what the dealers had been paying for the private brands.

"They all had to scramble," Galvin said. "They went to the customer who had been buying our private brands and sold him sets at half what he had been buying our sets for. The dealers knew they were better off buying brand names at a substantial discount and maybe it helped reduce the inventory of the big fellows, but it sure didn't help the small manufacturer like myself.

"I found myself with a lot of parts ordered I had no use for, and my customers with an inventory of my radios they wanted to send back. I went to the supplier to cancel what I no longer needed, but he was committed to his parts people.

It was a period of compromise and negotiation, taking some, sending back some, and splitting the loss.''

By Christmas of 1929, Galvin was just about out of business again. To add to the burden of these months he was struck by personal tragedy.

His father, John Galvin, died October 8, 1929, in his sleep at the age of sixty-three. Shortly after his father's death, Galvin's mother, Alice Galvin, developed an acute nephritis and died December 9, 1929, at the age of fifty-eight—sixty-one days after her husband.

In August of that year, 1929, Galvin's mother-in-law, Mrs. Guinan, also had died. So within the space of five months, he lost his mother, father and mother-in-law. A man can endure this tragedy as Galvin did, but not without a grave acceptance of the truth of Ecclesiastes that all things are man's portion; that he might be given riches and wealth but that with this lot, there would be much sorrow. To an old friend not too many months before his own death, Galvin said sadly, ''I know something about death.''

Music
on Wheels
8

With the shattering of the private label radio
business in 1929, Galvin realized that he was once
more on the precipice of failure. He would have
had sufficient reason through those bitter days to
think that defeat would follow him all of his life.
He still had a shop with Joe, and a few employees
that he would not be able to keep on the payroll
for very long unless something could be found to
manufacture and sell. Driven by necessity, struck
bold by desperation, and perhaps with a shade of
luck, he made his next major move.

"I was in New York working out a compromise with one of my suppliers on merchandise
I no longer needed when he mentioned there were
a couple of fellows over on Long Island making
custom installation of radios in cars. Just a back-
yard, garage-type operation. They would take the
dashboard off the car and build in a breadboard
chassis and stick it back of the panel. They drilled
holes so that the tuning knobs poked out the front
on the dashboard. They put a little aerial under
the running board or up into the header in the top
of the car, and a little four inch cone speaker
under the dash. He told me that all this, with
added provision for the bulky "B" batteries,
made the unit the devil to put in and the fellows
charged up to $240 for an installation.

"I thought about that back in the hotel and on
the train returning to Chicago, and it sparked the
idea in me of package car radios on a big scale
which had never been done. So I went back to our

shop and called Joe and all the boys together and said, 'Why can't we build an automobile radio that we can sell at a decent price? There's a full market for it and we're certainly not going to be flooded with merchandise there.' ''

There had been a few earlier attempts on the part of some of the men in the shop on their own at custom auto radio installations. One such instance had Hank Saunders, one of the early engineers, and a cab driver named Charley Horowitz, who spent much of his spare time around the shop, setting up an Atwater-Kent battery receiver in a metal box that acted as a shield on the back seat of Horowitz's Model A coupe. To improvise an antenna, they dropped the cloth in the top of the car, exposing the chicken wire. They cut two inches of the chicken wire around the edge of the top which left the bulk of the wire insulated from the car body. To restore rigidity, they laced the top back together with butcher twine.

The static noise reception they obtained was typical of the problems of installation which required finding a place for the receiver, the bulky "B" batteries and the speaker. Most important of all was the need to lick the excessively noisy ignition interference, and to obtain audio output of sufficient volume to override the noise of the auto in motion.

A couple of months of exhausting and relentless work now began in earnest. The clocks of a normal working day were discarded in a drive to

solve the frustrating problems. Numerous diagrams were drawn and torn up. Ideas were at-
tacked and defended with vigor and sometimes
vehemence. No innovation was too unconventional
to be tried. The men took turns working on one
another's cars and more than one car did not survive the operations.

It was a case of shoehorning parts into place
by drilling, sawing, bolting and remounting in
some instances a dozen times to gain a few precious inches of space. They worked during the day
on the street outside the Harrison plant with two
wheels of a car up on the curb so a man could get
underneath. They worked into the night by the
bobbing light of a mechanic's lamp.

When it rained they moved the car to the
service station of Red Silvers on nearby Jackson
Boulevard and into the shelter of his garage.
When a new installation had been completed, a
couple of men would take the car out for the crucial test under road conditions. After a while, to
keep from becoming disheartened, they stopped
keeping a record of the number of failures.

The matter was given an additional urgency
by Galvin's somewhat arbitrary decision that if
they were going to survive and get into any kind
of car radio production that year, they had to
have a working installation completed in time for
him to drive the car to the Radio Manufacturer's
Association Convention in Atlantic City in June
of 1930, approximately a month away. Galvin's

ungrounded optimism angered a number of his men and at least one was heard to mutter darkly that he was either "crazy or a plain damn fool." Joe Galvin, remembering the popcorn business in Harvard and the struggles of the battery company had a different version. "He doesn't know when he's licked," Joe would smile, "and until he does I won't admit I am." Then he drove himself and the men harder. They began experimenting on Galvin's Studebaker, saying, "if this installation doesn't work, P.V. will be walking to Atlantic City with the radio on his back."

Perhaps, because they had endured a good deal more than their share of disappointments, or simply that the long hours and hard work were beginning to produce results, they miraculously managed to complete a working test model on Galvin's car a few days before the convention. It was a far cry from the relatively effortless installations of present car radios, but it worked, the radio signal coming in clearly when the engine was running.

Cars in those days had no provision of any kind for the insertion of a bulky metal radio case the size of a fishing tackle box, a second large box housing the batteries and a third box housing the loud speaker, as well as the wiring for the batteries, antenna, and speaker.

They finally found a place for the radio under the hood by some remarkable shoehorning. They had to drill holes through the firewall and run a

pair of tuning shafts through them. The set was
tuned by a variable condenser. The tuning knobs
were in a sheet metal box clamped to the steering
wheel column inside the car. Between the radio under the hood and the control panel out front, they
ran solid steel shafts with universal joints. One
shaft tuned from station to station and the other
turned the set on and off and regulated the volume.
To house the "B" batteries, a hole was cut in the
floor of the car and the battery box lodged there
with special care taken to miss the muffler, drive
shaft, and frame members.

The set was in and worked. It remained to be
seen whether it would continue to work as well
under road conditions. Galvin took Lillian and
their son Bob, who was a few months short of
eight, and started the trip to Atlantic City.

It was a severe test for the new radio installation. Roads were still a long way from the
smooth stretches of superhighway that would
enter in the 50s and 60s. There were patches of
pavement followed abruptly by miles of gravel.
The gravel roads had "washboards" at crucial
points, a series of wavey bumps that could strike
a massive jolt into any automobile.

Galvin began the trip with apprehension that
the radio would have ceased functioning by the
time they arrived in Atlantic City. The gravest
difficulties that developed were directly traceable
to the long solid tuning rods connecting the set
with its controls. When Galvin hit the stretches of

gravel, the steering shaft of the car vibrated one way and the body vibrated another. Since the radio tuning controls were mounted on the steering column, and the set itself was mounted some 24 to 30 inches distant under the dashboard, the long solid tuning shafts transmitted every shimmy and shake of the road into a kind of "galloping modulation" that made singers sound as if they were vocalizing under water.

But they arrived in Atlantic City with the set still working. Galvin had no booth, no appointments and no convention space allotted to him for demonstration purposes. With Lillian helping him, he set up a position for the car at a little circular parkway running between Park Place and Indiana Avenue which ran adjacent to the Boardwalk. This allowed Galvin to collar dealers from the convention who happened to be strolling along the Boardwalk and induce them to get in the car and make a short turn around the small square to listen to the performance of the radio. Sometimes, while he went to locate another dealer, Lillian demonstrated the radio with a fervor that almost matched Galvin's.

When activity on the Boardwalk slowed down, he entered the Convention Hall and approached a number of the dealers, trying to draw them outside to take a ride. Many scoffed, unwilling to allow him even a few moments. A few went out with him and returned impressed. At the same time that they recognized the installation as ingenious most of them could not envision the development as one of any special significance on a large scale.

Meanwhile, unknown to Galvin, his activities were being watched with some interest and word spread among the conventioners that he was a "bootlegger from Chicago." Galvin was suddenly surprised to find himself the center of considerable attention and for a few moments he was allowed to jubilantly feel that his campaign was beginning to spark fire. This euphoria was quickly dispelled when several men began to ask the same question. "Where's the booze?"

Although the trip to Atlantic City was not marked by any immediate or enthusiastic success, it was a creditable beginning. A number of dealers convinced as much by Galvin as they were by the demonstration ordered one or two sets. A few bought more, the largest order being for six sets. The total number was small but still sufficient to send Galvin back to Chicago more than ever convinced there was a future for him in car radio.

The primary task facing the lab and shop in Chicago was to get as many trouble-free sets into cars as they could. A major problem was to find a way to replace the solid tuning shafts that had caused Galvin so much grief on the trip.

What was needed was a flexible shaft, something as easy and limber to work with as a piece of wire—yet one that would drive the tuning condenser and volume control in the set when the control knobs were turned up front.

Up to that time flexible shafts were used only for sheep clippers, dental drills, and barber clippers, but even these were made to turn only in one direction. The radio tuning shafts would have to work equally well in both directions so the radio controls could be moved either way.

Galvin established contact with a dental supply house that imported such flexible shafts for dental drills. Their cost was extremely high and added greatly to the expense of the installation. Besides it was doubtful whether they could ever be obtained in the quantities that Galvin felt would be needed for expanded production.

Galvin happened to mention the serious problem quite in passing to the cashier at his bank one day. By a strange and inexplicable quirk of fate, the banker had talked only a few days before to a manager of a washing machine company that used such a flexible shaft. They had ordered a huge quantity of them made in Germany and upon arrival in Chicago, they were found to be unsuitable because they were the wrong length. But they could not be returned and constituted dead inventory.

Galvin followed this lead although he had little confidence that the problem could be solved by such uncanny luck. But as Elmer Wavering remembers, "They were exactly what we would have ordered. The shaft was perfect for length, diameter, bushings and everything else. We bought the entire stock from the washing machine company at a liquidation price. The first sets we sent out were equipped with these new shafts.''

Galvin later retold this story on more than one occasion to lightly make the point that good luck sometimes had as much to do with success as hard work. In a more serious mood he told his son in private, ''Some people call it luck but no one will ever convince me that the Lord wasn't looking over my shoulder at that moment to guide me in the right direction.''

Many serious problems remained. One that required endless experimentation came in the matter of the installation.

''In those days we didn't have steel automobiles with a solid metal top,'' Wavering said. ''The car bodies were 'composite' made of sheet metal fastened over wooden frames, with tops of fabric stretched over chicken wire and wood.

''The single pole aerial hadn't been developed yet and we had to put plenty of aerial wire into the car. To install the aerial we had to strip the upholstery material out of the top of the car, and then snip the netting in the roof to get it away from all the metals. Otherwise it would serve as the ground and the set wouldn't work.

''If somebody bought a new car and decided to put in a car radio they'd get a real shock. They saw us go in and rip out the brand new head-lining in the car, drill holes into the floor for our batteries, and rig up a whole complicated electrical system with a network of wires. It took a minimum of eight hours to install a set and if we ran into trouble, it could run into several days.''

Besides the challenge of mounting the separate radio unit, loud speaker, batteries, control head and antenna in the many different models of early cars, these six or more units had to be connected to each other with a system of control and connector cables and leads.

If all these mountings and connections had been successfully accomplished, the radio might deliver some music—if the car was standing still and with the engine turned off. When the car's engine was started, a crescendo of ''ignition noise'' would crackle and sizzle to drown out the music.

Spark plug and distributor ''suppressors'' were commonly used in an effort to minimize the spark interference that radiated from these parts. ''In the beginning,'' recalls Elmer Wavering, ''we often had to use so many suppressors that the engine wouldn't start, or if it started, it would die out when you tried to pick up speed.''

Besides the four, six or eight spark plug suppressors and distributor suppressor, the 1930 installations also required a generator condenser, a ''hash'' filter choke, a dome-light filter, two or more hood wipers, several grounding straps, and four wheel static springs, plus an infinite cut and try patience.

But with each installation the Galvin engineers and service men learned some answers to these problems by trial and error. By this persistent troubleshooting an improvement in performance and ease of installation was achieved. The Motorola trademark in these first years earned the reputation of "America's finest car radio."

By 1935 the Galvin engineers had perfected a "Magic Eliminode" circuit, wherein the interfering signal was reversed in phase and then fed back into the antenna. The reversed signal actually cancelled the spark noise and thus eliminated the need for any spark plug suppressors.

But this was still in the future. Back in 1930 the hours of work were long and the funds were low. Money for working capital was a constant source of concern. In the course of negotiations with a leading bank, Galvin suggested installing a radio in one of the banker's cars as a practical demonstration of the soundness of car radio.

On a day that the final loan papers were signed Wavering and Saunders headed a team that worked with fervor to make the installation on the banker's new Packard. Several times in the course of the work Galvin emerged from his office with the bankers, explaining some phase of the operation and carrying on at some length about the grand and imposing future of music on wheels.

Philip and Helen,
youngest of
the five Galvin children

Growing up,
young Paul

High-school
sweethearts:
Lillian and Paul, 1913

Camp Bowie, Texas

Officer candidate graduate

After being skinned by the barber, all
shavetails looked about alike on I.D. cards

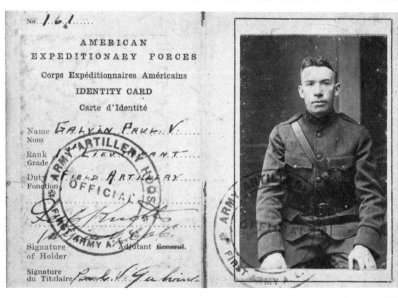

Paul and
son Bob,
Chicago, 1924

At age four,
Bob decided
to be a doctor

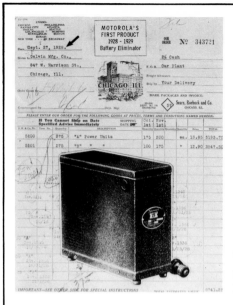

The Battery Eliminator:
first product,
1928–29

The Harrison
Street plant,
1928-1937

When the installation was complete the crew stood by grinning in triumph as the radio was turned on and worked perfectly.

A considerable amount of time was spent in the exchange of hearty congratulations. The bankers swept away in a cloud of good will. Wavering and Saunders, assembling their tools and cleaning up, paid little attention a short while later to a fire engine wailing by the shop. The neighborhood was a heavily populated one and fires were not unusual. It wasn't long, however, before word was carried to them that the car on which they had just made the installation was on fire a few blocks away. Along with a shaken Galvin they hurried to the scene of the fire in time to see the firemen soaking down the smoking remains of the banker's Packard. The agitated bankers explained how a few moments after leaving the shop they noticed the first sign of smoke curling from beneath the hood. They had curbed the car and jumped out and called the fire department from a nearby grocery.

Galvin talked to them with a mighty and desperate eloquence in an attempt to console and reassure them. They must have felt considerable anxiety about the whole episode, and this had a sobering effect upon the entire shop for several weeks.

"We were never sure just what caused it," Saunders said, "but the timing was humiliating. If it had happened at least a few days later, but it was less than thirty minutes after we finished.''

Fires were, while not too frequent, a hazard of those early experiments. The men in the shop used their own cars for bold and untried innovations and on more than one occasion needed water buckets and a hose.

Galvin fared as gravely as the others. There was an early afternoon when a crew working on his car broke for lunch. It was not long before one of the men who had become as sensitive as firehouse dogs to the scent of smoke noticed a tiny spiral curling from under the hood of Galvin's car. He shouted and ran for water. A number of men hurried to help at about the same time that Galvin came in agitation from his office.

"Whose car is it?" Galvin shouted coming down the stairs.

His ownership was soon established and Galvin struggled between an understanding of the benefits of research and innovation and the worn patience of a man being asked to do more than his share. Finally he could not contain himself and cried. "Damn it! That's the second time for my car this month!"

But Galvin fully appreciated the complexity of the problems facing them and encouraged his men to think boldly, whether the consequences led to fire or not. Unlike those executives who seek to mold men into their own image, he believed in giving his men the latitude to show what they could do largely on their own.

He could take his turn in the shop with them, sharing, as Joe did, their frustrations and success. While he was not an engineer, on more than one occasion he provided a key to solving a knotty problem by his ability to cut away the superfluous. "Now let's use our nutpickers on this problem," he would say quietly, "and then we'll decide what it is we have to do. Then let's do it."

Because he had a strange steadfast belief in himself, he could inspire his men with the feeling that nothing was impossible. His faith in them made them wish to prove him right, and, as a consequence, they often did superbly what at first they did not think they could do at all.

More Than
a Brother
9

The original model 5T71 auto radio that Galvin carried to Atlantic City established the first of the many "Motorola Firsts" in product design that were to follow. This model sold for $110 to $130 with accessories, including installation. It was designed to fit any of the popular cars of that period, and designed so that it could be produced on a commercial basis. It has justifiably been called the "First Commercial Auto Radio."

A few other companies and individuals had designed, manufactured, and marketed an automobile radio as far back as 1927, according to Dunlap's Radio Almanac. But these auto radios were "custom" designed for a specific installation. They were made and sold on an "as ordered" basis at a price of $200 to $300. Installing these sets meant rebuilding the dashboard as well as the body top and B battery space.

The original Galvin model also established several other firsts in the use of a steering column control head and Electrodynamic loud speaker. Later in 1930, there was also the push-pull audio amplifier used in another model. One of the 1932 models was the first auto radio to use a superheterodyne circuit. It was also the first auto radio made available with a separate B Battery Eliminator. In the same year, the self-contained "Elkonode" B Power Supply for the model 88 was a big "Motorola First."

During 1930, Galvin Manufacturing Corporation began selling the first models to be marketed under the Motorola label, a name that suggested both motion and radio, which seemed to Galvin striking and effective. The name Motorola had come to Galvin quite simply as an inspiration one morning while he was shaving.

But many of the shipments during this same period were unlabeled sets, sold as the earlier home radios had been sold, with the dealer or distributor affixing his own label. While this distressed him, Galvin had neither the money nor the organization to demand recognition of his corporate or new trade name "Motorola." But he also knew that the best kind of advertising were the radios themselves. Each set installed and operating became a "rolling demonstrator" that attracted many other potential customers within earshot along the street.

Yet, infuriated complaints about the difficulties of installing the radios continued to come in from the field.

"Nobody around here knows how to put one of these sets into the car," a dealer calling Galvin from Texas said angrily. "How the hell can we sell them if nobody can install them?"

Galvin knew that their degree of success in overcoming this lack of information might well determine whether the struggling company could survive. Without any sales or service organization to throw into the breach, he enlisted Elmer Wavering and himself to travel through the country, both selling car radios and holding sessions

on their installation. They planned a campaign
that would bring him into cities a few days ahead
of Wavering. Galvin would obtain an order for
radios with a solemn promise that, "our Mr.
Wavering will follow up within a few days to provide your people a complete lesson in installation
and maintenance." When Wavering arrived in
town, the groups were ready for his presentation.
Later, in 1931, Galvin and Wavering would be
joined on the road by Bill Engle, Murray Yeo-
mans, Dale Andrews, and Johnny Rogers. This
nucleus of an organization helped establish the
first Authorized Motorola Installation Stations
that would, within the space of just a few years,
develop a countrywide army of men able to skill-
fully install car radios.

But for the first months most of the burden
rested on the backs of Galvin and Wavering. If
either of them got back home, it was only briefly,
long enough to maintain some contact with the
developments in the shop. Earl McGowan, then in
charge of shipping, would remember nights after
the shop closed when Galvin would return from a
trip and come in to drop his traveling bags
wearily in the corner of his office.

"He'd just come in off the road," McGowan
recalled, "but he'd work there in the shop with
Joe, probably until two or three o'clock in the
morning just getting his records and orders
straight so that he could leave again sometime the
next day."

William James speaks of the "once-born" and the "twice-born." The "once-born" he defined as those who early in life know who they are, what they need, and where they want to go. The "twice-born" are those who, sometime in later life, have to shed their skins and become in a way reborn. Their search for identity and stability is often painful to themselves and to others.

Galvin was certainly one of those who were "once-born." He never doubted that his destiny was to have a successful business of his own. He pursued this aim with a relentlessness of purpose that was sometimes disconcerting to those around him. In most lives, experience is taken as it comes and left to rest in the memory where it happens to fall. Galvin never took anything just as it came. The thing that happened to him was merely the point of departure for a greater concentration of effort. His life contained a cycle of energy and purpose that was indeed remarkable.

He was fortunate in having Lillian, a wife able to share his dreams and understand that he labored for her and their son as much as for himself. From Harvard to Marshfield and then to Chicago, she had known little in the way of material security. She was a lovely woman who enjoyed gaiety and dancing, and in those difficult early years there was little time for anything but work. But all this work and the loneliness of the weeks that Galvin was away she endured with a serene and unusual patience.

Galvin was also fortunate in having Joe. As he traveled the country, he could rest securely in the fact that Joe was running the shop, backing him up, getting the things done that needed to be done. If Joe had had his choice, he would probably have been a policeman, since he had a great respect and admiration for policemen.

Although the brothers had a great loyalty and affection for one another, all his life, until his premature death in 1944, Joe would be trying to match Galvin in work and purpose. Not as far-seeing as his older brother, perhaps not quite as able a businessman, he had less of Galvin's reserve and in his own right was a lively and spirited man of great wit. From the days of the Stewart Battery Company in Marshfield, Joe was determined to keep up with his brother. He drove himself hard and on nights when the pressures and tensions needed release Joe would go along with some of the men in the shop for a long evening of companionship and some hard drinking. But he was on the job in the morning and expected the rest of the men to be there as well.

Joe's contribution to the growth and development of the company was a tremendous one. His work and his personality and his warm and earnest temperament did much to soothe areas of friction which Galvin's sometimes arbitrary demands might create. In the very early months of the new company, when Galvin fell considerably behind in payment to a number of suppliers, the

Credit Committee of the Radio Manufacturers Association considered a court order to foreclose on the assets of the struggling company.

It was Joe Galvin who sat down with the members of the RMA committee and in a series of meetings prevailed upon them to go along and hold off any action. He accomplished this concession by informing the members fully and openly of the affairs of the company and the direction in which it was moving.

Galvin and Joe complemented each other effectively. Galvin was basically a negotiator, tough when he had to be, but fair and courteous. He had a marked ability to impress people with his sincerity. Once having sold a supplier on the quality of his word and his character Galvin would ask for a letter, "explaining that you have agreed to extend me credit on this amount of material until such a date." This letter then became a solid wedge in his approach to another company.

Once Galvin had pledged his word it became a matter of honor to see that word fulfilled. Joe made sure that all orders and schedules were met by a constant vigil over the working of the plant. "Paul promised these units for next Monday," he would tell his men. "Now let's get them out well before and not let him down."

Later on in the unsuccessful attempts to organize the Motorola plants, it was the great respect of the men in the shop for Joe as well as

Galvin that made them decide to cast their lot with the future of the company.

On March 7, 1944, Lewis Ingram, the Detroit distributor, on a trip to the company offices on Augusta Boulevard found Frank Dunn, the watchman, an employee for many years, with tears running down his cheeks.

"What is the matter?" Ingram asked.

"Joe is dead," Frank Dunn said. "Our Joe is dead."

To the present day, twenty years after his death, numerous photographs of Joe hang beside those of Galvin above the work tables and on the office walls of the older employees, a moving reminder of the affection in which both men are held.

Tell Them the Truth

10

In the first months of 1931, the country twisted in the economic spider web of the depression. The unemployment statistics of this period could not begin to reveal the extent of the problem in terms of human suffering and despair. On his sales trips to develop markets for auto radio, Galvin saw bread lines and soup kitchens in more than one city and entire families lined up for their meagre ration. He witnessed demonstrations as men marched with banners demanding food and work. In several instances, he saw the demonstrations erupt into violence and this convinced him of the revolutionary temper sweeping the unemployed and destitute of the land.

"It was a bad time," he recalled. "The big hungry eyes of children in the soup lines tore out your heart."

Although he was a Republican, bound to that tradition by his small town and midwestern upbringing, he knew that the times, the anger and the fear demanded stringent measures to relieve the situation. He felt it a personal reflection on all American business that free enterprise proved insufficient to avert the catastrophe or to fill the tremendous vacuum of unemployment. He spent many hours discussing the problem with commercial travelers whom he met in the small hotels in various cities where he spent the night.

"When we come out of this depression," he said to a friend, "we will never again be able to return completely to the old beliefs in the self-

97

regulating character of the economy. More and
more I am afraid we are going to find ourselves
drawn under the direction of government.''

He returned home disheartened by what he
had seen, suspecting that much worse was still to
come. Yet he still argued hotly against those
gloomy extremists who saw the depression as the
forerunner of total economic collapse. He submit-
ted the condition of his own business as a good au-
gur for the recovering of the economy in general.

Although Galvin Manufacturing had ended
the year of 1930 with a deficit of only $3,745 on a
sales record of $287,000, the only deficit in the
company's history to date, the business was actually stronger than at any time since its inception.
The factory had grown to cover two full floors of
the Harrison Street building, and the men, hard-
ened by experience and adversity into a versatile
and aggressive team, were ready to try anything.
The auto radio installation centers in various
parts of the country reported a mounting interest
in the product and orders had begun to come into
the factory at an increasing rate.

The demand for the 1931 models, while not
huge in terms of orders, required a still further
expansion of the production facilities of the company, and they took over another floor.

In that year the first Motorola distributor-
ships were established to become the nucleus of a
wholesale distributor organization, marked by
unusual vigor and success, with an impressive loy-

alty to the company and its products. Moore
Equipment in Dayton, Ohio, under the guidance of
"Dutch" Moore became the first Motorola distributor in January of 1931, to be followed in
February by Herb Wall in Ft. Wayne and Motor
Radio in Pittsburgh. Nate Cooper of New York
City, a zestful and enthusiastic man who had once
climbed a twenty-foot pole in a high wind to prove
a point about antenna reception to Galvin, joined
in April. Disco Distributing and Ralph Morrison
of St. Louis joined in May. Frank Kearns, Galvin's Atlantic City friend, who had very early
grasped the tremendous potential of auto radio,
joined in June. Porter Burgess was the last for
the year with his distributorship in Dallas.

With many of these men Galvin formed
friendships that remained close until his death.
Nate Cooper could say, "He helped make us
wealthy, but he made men out of some of us too."
"He made no wild promises," another man said,
"but he was a man with a vision that he made you
see, too."

In August of 1931, a slim and unassuming
young engineer named Ray Yoder joined the Galvin company. Within a year he spearheaded a
crew and was the single man most responsible for
a tremendously significant breakthrough in the
field of auto radio. This was the development of
a vibrator type power supply which replaced the
large, bulky and short-lived B batteries. This design achievement soon gave the Motorola brand

name a decisive lead in the auto radio field which
the company vigorously exploited.

With the growth of auto radio, agitation developed in a number of states for legislation
prohibiting the use of radios in automobiles on
the basis they constituted a hazardous distraction.
In the course of coroners' investigations into the
reasons for auto accidents, questions were asked
whether the auto contained a radio in operation
at the time.

Although no legislation was ever passed ban-
ning the use of radios in cars, a number of stern
efforts were launched to invoke such legislation.
The most active effort for legislation was made in
St. Louis, Missouri, on the grounds that radios in
autos were an "invitation to disaster." The Radio Manufacturers Association fought this legislation and Galvin journeyed to the hearings of the
City Council in St. Louis, and with the help of
Ralph Morrison spoke against the proposal. He
produced figures to prove that the rate of accidents remained virtually the same as it had been
before the introduction of car radios.

Another thorny problem, one that had
plagued the fledgeling company from the beginning, continued to be the matter of radio installation in autos. Although the establishment of the
installation centers had greatly improved the
situation, the number of trained people available
could not begin to meet the demand. A number of

"curbside operators," sensing the vast potential of the market for quick profit, entered the field with a screwdriver and a wrench. Inadequately trained to make the still difficult installations, their incompetency helped produce a rising chorus of grievance and complaint.

In an effort to combat this problem, Galvin and his men worked strenuously over a service manual which, when finally issued in late 1930, consisted of twenty-eight pages of fine, small print and eight crude diagrams. There were repeated reassurances in the text that "the installation of Motorola Auto-Radio is comparatively simple."

"It is merely a matter of understanding and taking pains," the manual went on soothingly, "together with observing and carrying out essential details." Then it continued with a moderately subtle euphemism to rouse the pride and ego of the purchaser. "While Motorola design effectively meets the requirements necessary for simple installation, the problems encountered in various makes of automobiles presents ample opportunity to exercise skillful ingenuity which makes installation interesting and enjoyable."

After reissue in 1931, the 1932 service manual was expanded to thirty-five pages of slightly smaller, closely spaced print compensated for by much better illustrations.

In the following year, Galvin Manufacturing suffered with the Model 55. The "infamous

Model 55," as it came to be known, was not the
only set designed that year, but it far overshad-
owed the other models in service problems.

"All of the Model 55s shipped to the field
bred troublesome pups," Wavering said. "The
power supply was underdesigned and in order to
make the model work successfully in the car, we
made the fatal mistake of connecting the wires
directly to the storage battery without a fuse.
This was done because the fuse produced a high
loud humming. With the model underpowered,
after a few hours operation, the vibrator would
stick, start to burn up the transformer, then the
wires, and finally the car."

The dreaded ogre of fire returned to haunt
them. An attorney in Sioux City, Iowa, had a
Model 55 installed in his car in his garage, which
was one of the first attached to the house. The
car burned and the garage burned and half
the house burned down. In another instance, a
Model 55 installed in a hearse set the vehicle on
fire and to the dismay of the family and friends
who preferred a more conventional funeral, the
hapless cadaver was cremated.

Finally, in desperation at the increasing number of complaints and angry denunciations that
rolled in from the field, Galvin recalled the several
thousand sets already shipped and salvaged the
tubes and speakers. He then had the sets destroyed. Joe Galvin wielded one of the sledge
hammers that did the job.

But Galvin would not let these reverses get him down. He had fought through hard and distressing years and had proven his ability to react decisively rather than merely respond to adversity. He could even see the humor in his plight.

"Smashing those sets gave us all a chance to let off steam," Galvin said. "It cleared the air. We needed some release because we were just getting on our feet. When those sets came back we were down again. It wouldn't have taken much more than that to keep us down. But I had been down a number of times and I knew I could get back up."

*   *   *   *

Through this period he made time for Sunday visits back to Harvard to spend the day with Burley and Helen and Lillian's relatives, the Deneen and Duggan families.

He drew a certain emotional sustenance from the scenes of his childhood, from the memories the quiet town recalled for him. He also thoroughly enjoyed the gathering of the families.

He was fond of aunt Rose Deneen, who spread an abundant table for what she lightly called her "city cousins." Uncle George Duggan was a masterful storyteller and he would tell and retell his favorite supply of Irish stories which Galvin delighted to hear. Galvin would match Duggan's tales with stories of his own assembled in his travels around the country. He too was a good storyteller, with a fine sense of timing, and the festive occasions were often beset by Galvin and uncle George humorously trying to equal and outdo each other in that ancient and sparkling Irish art. Galvin returned to his business with renewed and freshened spirit on Monday mornings.

The introduction of several really fine auto radio models in 1934 went a long way to dispel the unfortunate image created by the lethal Model 55.

In that year Motorola auto radios were produced which sold at $49.50, and at $64.50. Both of these models were beautifully designed and incorporated all that the engineers and Galvin had learned of auto radio through almost six years of trial and error. They accomplished the feat of increasing the audio output without also increasing the amplified noise and distortion. For the first time the units had sufficient power to produce a rich true bass tone, and were also marked by a high degree of sensitivity, with an ability to bring in weak signals loud and clear.

In the autumn of 1934, Elmer Wavering was recalled from the field. There had been some trouble with a sales manager, and when Wavering received a cryptic telegram from Galvin asking him to come home, he anticipated the worst. He found instead that Galvin was making him his assistant with a considerable measure of added responsibility. Knowing that Wavering was fully informed of the problems in the field, Galvin desired a closer liaison between those problems and the engineering program.

By this time, the tremendous potential of mass-produced auto radios had become apparent to the radio industry and many of the larger firms launched campaigns to compete for the market.

One of the major competitors, in a bold drive to achieve domination of the field, came out with a four-tube radio with a single bolt mounting, and, to the tune of a massive advertising campaign, released tens of thousands of sets awakening the whole country to the joy of auto radio listening. But without the years of research in auto radio application which Galvin had experienced, it would have been difficult for any company, however large and efficient, to have foreseen or anticipated the incredible range of problems that were possible.

The four-tube sets proved inadequate under field conditions and the complaints became a great and fervent chorus. This proved a tremendous boon to Galvin, because they were able to capitalize on the competitor's massive advertising campaign which had made the entire country more conscious of the delights of "music while you ride." While the inadequacies of the four-tube set must have soured a good many buyers on car radio in general, in many other instances the model was pulled out and replaced with a Motorola—a proven and dependable product.

As car radio began to catch the public atten-

tion, some retailers began to dream up original
selling approaches. They tied the purchase of a
car radio to a deceptively hazy set of conditions.
One Chicago dealer offered a car radio free of
charge if the buyer simply recommended ten other
prospects. The only catch in this display of generosity was that all ten of the recommended prospects had to buy radios at the listed price. Since
the dealer had taken a chattel mortgage on the
original purchaser's car, it left him in a position
to press at once for full payment of the obligation.

Galvin was outraged at these tactics and
countered them in many ways. He sought to demonstrate success with respectable methods of merchandising. The most fruitful of these was the development of a progressive relationship with the
B. F. Goodrich Company, and through its hun-
dreds of branches and stores provide its reliable
and trustworthy installment plan for those Motorola customers wishing to finance their purchase.

This was a "cornerstone" relationship for
the young company. It was based on the respect
that developed between Galvin and the managers
of this tire company—managers whom Galvin
came to regard as some of the most qualified men
he was to know throughout his career.

As the years went on, this supplementary
pattern of distribution—Goodrich served by
Motorola through its wholesale distributors—

was one of the many reasons for the success and growth of the Motorola consumer products.

* * * *

That year, 1934, was also marked by the full time affiliation with Galvin of a remarkable advertising innovator named Victor Irvine.

He was a small, zestful and dynamic man with bright, humorous eyes. He had been around in a semiofficial capacity since 1930. In that year, through a friend of his who worked at Galvin Mfg., he was asked to come over and help "without pay but merely to keep me out of mischief."

In the beginning, he did some writing, got out a small monthly paper that contained some novel selling ideas and trade chatter. In about a month, he went on the payroll at $10 a week, hardly a munificent sum even in those lean days. After several months, he left to take a job in advertising offered to him elsewhere, but he continued to shuttle back and forth, having found in Galvin and his associates a congenial group of sales-minded engineers and merchandisers. He would leave the office in which he worked and meet them daily, usually at the Fred Harvey Union Depot lunchroom, and in this way was kept informed of the company's fortunes.

Irvine was in charge of the first national advertising display presentations for Motorola. It was a very modest beginning of one column ads on page three running once a month in the now de-

funct *Collier's* and in the *Saturday Evening Post*.
But Irvine introduced them to the distributors
with the pomp and pageantry reserved for the
crowning of a Roman Caesar. He engaged Little
Johnny, the famous midget who did the Philip
Morris cigarette commercials and who worked as
a bellboy for the Edgewater Beach Hotel in
Chicago.

Against a carefully lighted stage, a great
blowup on cardboard of the coming ad seemed to
glide onto the stage by itself. In reality, of course,
it was being carried in by Little Johnny hidden
behind the placard. He then backed out and scur-
ried around the backdrop to bring out another
placard from the other side of the stage and then
back out again unseen.

The program might appear modest and a little tame by present-day standards when great and
flamboyant spectacles rivaling Broadway musi-
cals are the accepted pattern at the sales and
marketing meetings of the larger companies, but
for its time the program was bold and animated.
The effect on the distributors was electrifying.
They shouted, whistled, stamped, and clapped at
the announcement of national advertising and at
the novelty of the presentation.

Irvine was also primarily responsible for the
great Motorola highway advertising program
which had thousands of red, yellow and black
signs blazing the Motorola name along highways
across the country. Children on auto excursions

with their parents played games by counting the signs which appeared to be everywhere. The signs did a memorable job of inexpensively advertising Motorola products.

But in certain instances the signs produced unexpected results. The hunters of Nebraska, Illinois and Iowa could not withstand the appeal of knocking out the neat line of o's in Motorola. One disgruntled Iowan, perhaps unhappy at his inaccuracy from a distance, took a shotgun and blazed away at close range to all but destroy the name completely.

In Florida, a week after fifty signs had been erected, ominous word was received that they had all mysteriously disappeared. An investigating force was dispatched. After several days of exploration they found that the Seminole Indians had confiscated the signs and were using the heavy steel panels for the floors of their homes, standing them on piles 6 feet over the Everglades. Irvine asked Galvin for permission to let the Seminoles keep them, but arranged a peace treaty with the chief to prevent further confiscations. Still another unforeseen application came in various depression Jungletowns when the hobos built their shanties with the Motorola signs.

Galvin was impressed with the vitality and creativity of Irvine's ideas and left the advertising program pretty much to him. In 1937, Motorola, having filled the six floors of the Harrison Street building and overflowing into the

Cracker Jack building across the street, built its new offices and plant on Augusta Blvd. At that time, Irvine, who had operated as a consultant/agency man, came aboard officially as advertising manager. After a couple of months with a pair of file cabinets and boxes set around a desk for privacy he moved into a fashionable office on Mahogany Row. Months went by. He had not been paid since starting as an employee and one day asked Joe "whether employees were paid annually or semi-annually?" Investigation revealed that Irvine had been in and out of the offices for so long that nobody in payroll actually believed he had been officially hired.

"We had no precedent for what we did at Motorola," Irvine said. "It was hard work but rewarding. We tried whatever we wanted to try that looked and sounded right. We made mistakes, too, but we corrected them when we found out and tried not to repeat the same mistakes."

How well they succeeded was evidenced at one distributor's meeting when a cynical old merchandiser came up to Irvine and said, "I've been to many of these ballyhoos but this is the first one where no one tried to fool me. I don't know whether it's just that you guys are so dumb you don't know how to be dishonest or are just plain nuts. Anyway, I'm going back home and have my men sell hell out of your products."

Obviously, it was not that they were plain dumb. They would not have been able to survive the trying and competitive years without a real sagacity, but the standards which Galvin insisted be maintained required they play fair with their distributors and inform them honestly of the company situation and products.

"Tell them the truth," Galvin said, "first because it's right and second they'll find out anyway. If they don't find it out from us we'll be the ones to suffer."

Over the years Irvine gained a license to be impertinent in talking back to Galvin which very few other men in the company shared. They sometimes disagreed and were not averse to shouting at each other in an attempt to reach agreement. Galvin admired Irvine's capacity to shout. Once, hearing him hollering over the telephone from his own office further down Mahogany Row, he sent a gravely worded memo to Irvine suggesting that all his future long distance calls be made merely by opening the window in Irvine's office.

While there were many instances of humor between the two men and often areas of disagreement, Galvin was grateful and appreciative of Irvine's considerable contribution. Once, after Irvine had returned from a trip, Galvin saw him filling out an expense statement and told him sternly, "Never mind that business. When you go on a trip you just figure what you spent and collect it." He also made a solemn promise to Irvine that, "I'll never fire you or let you quit."

"People:
Exclamation Point"
11

In 1934, another man destined to make a considerable contribution to the company joined Galvin. Frank O'Brien, a hard driving man who had worked for another radio manufacturer until the company's failure during the depression, met Joe Galvin and impressed him. Joe offered O'Brien a job in purchasing. They spent two hours arguing whether O'Brien would get the $40 a week he was asking or the $22.50 that Joe offered him.

"I decided I would take the $22.50," O'Brien laughed, "inasmuch as Joe was not going to give me the $40. I didn't find out until some years later that at that time Paul and Joe Galvin were only taking about $30 a week out of the business themselves."

O'Brien recalled his first actual contact with Galvin.

"We used a varnished sleeving for insulation purposes in those days. We called it spaghetti because it came in long lengths and was round and hollow. I hadn't been working for the company very long when all of a sudden this stranger I had never met stormed in on me and said in a loud voice, 'This better be the last time we run out of spaghetti because spaghetti is like sugar in a grocery store and there is no damn reason to run out of either one.' "

A distinctive characteristic about Galvin, borne out by others beside O'Brien who knew him well, was his voice. It was deep and resonant and

112

could artfully ornament an emotional range from
anger to gentleness. He had a sense of presence, a
certain grave dignity, and when this gravity was
added to his voice, it made it easy for him to domi-
nate a meeting, or a roomful of men. O'Brien's
early experiences with Galvin were not always
happy ones. He enjoyed their association and
was impressed by the company but he was disturbed at times by Galvin's inconsistency on
minor problems.

"I lived at Long Avenue and Diversey,"
O'Brien said, "and in order to get to the Harrison Street building I had to take a Diversey bus
to Milwaukee and a Milwaukee Street car to
Logan Square and a Logan Square elevated to
Halsted Street, and then walk about five or six
blocks. One night, we had a terrific snowstorm and
I remember getting up two hours earlier than
usual because I knew traffic would be jammed.
When I got off at Halsted Street, it was about ten
minutes to nine and we were due in those days at
eight o'clock. So I ran like the very devil with my
trousers tucked into my socks and by tremendous
effort made it by nine.

"The switchboard operator let me know that
Mr. Galvin wanted me. I got in his office still out
of breath. He started bawling hell out of me because I was late. I ended up blowing up myself
and reminding him that for several weeks we had
been working fourteen to sixteen hours a day including Holy Days of Obligation. My office was on

the fourth floor and when I left his office I was so mad I slammed the door. As I started up the stairs I began to cool down and when I finally reached the fourth floor I was sorry. Later that day I followed him into his office and told him I was sorry I had lost my temper. He looked at me with that funny little smile playing around the corners of his mouth and said quietly, 'I don't even remember talking to you about that.' "

The paradoxical quality of Galvin's anger was that it was occasionally vented upon a person unjustly, but when the inconsistency was pointed out to him, he would give the impression that he had banished the entire episode from his mind. Others came to realize that although there wasn't a clear apology, he would clear the episode from his consciousness.

When it came to his own business mistakes he managed to convince his associates that he was not infallible. They learned they could go to him and say, "Paul, your decision yesterday was wrong." If the new facts, or an analysis they supplied, stood the test of his scrutiny, he would waste no more time on it.

"Tell the fellows we're changing. My decision yesterday was wrong."

Results were what he was after. These could only, he often said, follow the right decisions regardless of when, or how, or by whom these decisions were arrived at. He was particularly impatient of those men who could not admit their own business mistakes.

He had a unique way of adding up a man's potential in his own mind. Someone once said of him "that he could remember a mistake a man had made ten years before." It was true that he could recall these episodes of error, but what he watched closely were the ways in which the man either benefited or did not benefit from the mistakes. One of his favorite sayings was, "I don't mind a fellow who is dumb but I can't stand one who is numb."

Sometimes, he unleashed his anger to scourge a man he felt had been incompetent. More often, he used it as a prod to shock an able man into awareness that he was being lax or careless. If he felt it might help, he took drastic action to set the man back on the right road. "As far as I am concerned," he would say to the man in private, "you're out of a job as of now, fired. But we'll gamble a while longer. If you try to do this, we will do this." This talk was strong medicine and often very effective.

Employees could speak with awe at feeling the full force of his anger, which he reserved for moments of monumental aggravation. "He didn't cut you piece by piece," one man said. "He let go a blast like an explosion that struck you all at once and left your eyebrows and hair singed and your senses rattled."

In his later years, there was considerable speculation that much of this anger was calculated. A supplier remembered once how, after hearing Galvin rage against several assistants, he turned to the supplier, when the assistants had fled from the office, and, winking, said, "That should keep them moving for a while."

"The first time he let go at you like that," one of his men said, "you went back to your office and started to empty your desk. When you met him in the hall an hour later, he would astonish you by stopping and inquiring pleasantly about your family."

With his capacity for strong criticism, he was reserved with his praise. When a man had done something that pleased him, he acknowledged it gravely, but there was no effusive offering of compliments. Most of the men who worked closely with him accepted this stern standard, but at times there were ruffled feelings, complaints that he expected too much.

But in a lasting, yet not clearly defined way, he was able to generate tremendous loyalty in his men. Many would acknowledge frankly that he had inspired the course of their lives and men sought to model themselves after him, after his qualities of character and determination.

One of the most important reasons for the loyalty he developed was the fact that he was honest with people, did not hold himself above them, and placed great emphasis upon their dignity as human beings. He was pleased to reward initiative and agreed that authority rightly belonged to the person who boldly assumed responsibility.

His concern for people extended beyond the perimeters of their employment. Hearing of an illness in the family of one of his employees, he would call and inquire, "Are you sure you have got the best doctor? If there is any question, I know a physician right here in the city, the best man for a condition like that. I will be very glad to call him for you if you like." Through his efforts, many specialists were brought in who would have not been available otherwise. The procedure in these cases was to have the physician send the bill directly to him.

He took a personal interest in the problem of employee alcoholism. He would call the man in, talk to him, and try to get him to accept qualified medical help to straighten himself out. Once, when a supervisor recommended that a man be fired as a hopeless case, Galvin asked to talk to the man first. Twenty years later that particular employee was still employed and a supervisor himself.

Another instance of Galvin's concern for his people came during one of his walks through the shop when he saw a group of girls on one of the lines bundled up in overcoats as they worked. He queried the shop foreman as to the reason for it, and was told that since they were only working a single line with the rest of the shop down they were cutting the cost by conserving fuel and heat.

"I don't care if there is one girl working, or ten, or one hundred," Galvin answered sternly. "You treat them all alike and don't save money by abusing anyone."

Numerous stories of Joe Galvin's generosity also linger in the plants of Motorola. A girl on one of the production lines whose father, not a Motorola employee, was stricken with cancer was sent home on full pay to care for him. There were other instances of Joe advancing money from his own pocket to aid in paying the college tuition of an employee's son or daughter, or the expense of childbirth for an employee's wife. These acts of generosity were not merely predicated upon extreme hardship cases.

Bill Arnos, a young buyer in purchasing in the thirties, recalls that during the worst of the depression he put off much needed work on his teeth because he could not afford it. Joe saw him suffering and brusquely gave him the name of his own dentist and told him to go see him. When the work was done, the cost was a couple of hundred dollars, an incredible amount of money for the average wage earner in those days. Arnos never saw a bill and each query directed to Joe brought the laconic answer, "I will let you know."

A few years later, under better circumstances, Arnos told Joe frankly that he wanted to reimburse him for the bill that by then he knew Joe had paid. When Joe asked him why he was so concerned about it, Arnos replied that paying his bill

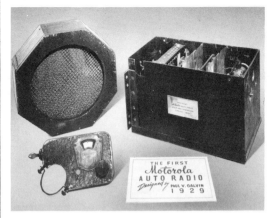

The car radio
product that
"put music
on wheels"

Typical shop
facilities at
Harrison plant
in the 1930s

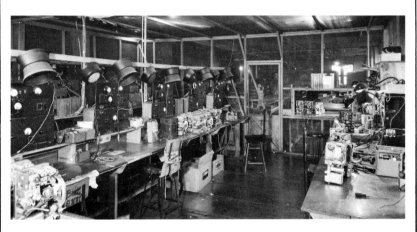

Below: The second annual dinner of the Motorola Service Club, December, 1939. From left to right: Ed Briscoe, Frank Petritis, Helen Lagowski, Harry Wawrzyniak, Johnny Hummel, Paul Galvin, Joe Galvin, Virginia Massarachia, Don Mitchell, Carl Zehnle, Opal Hamilton, and Joe Petritis. (Missing is Earl McGowan.) Several remain in the company in positions of responsibility.

The brothers, Paul and Joe

Elmer Wavering, then manager of the Auto Radio Division

Hugo Kraenzle with Paul and Joe
at "You can bake your own cake" distributors' convention

Relaxation on a trip
to Europe in
the mid-thirties

At Lakelawn resort,
Lake Delavan,
Wisconsin

A Sunday visit to see
Aunt Helen Kehoe

Florida, 1939

would allow Joe to concentrate on fixing some other employee's teeth.

Another example of Galvin's willingness to share his good fortune with others was the matter of bonuses. After the first few years of hard and desperate struggle, when the business finally began to improve, Galvin told the men who had been with him from the beginning he felt they should share in the rising fortune of the company beyond their salaries. He wanted them to understand they had an equity in the future of the company which would afford a man some security.

"I do not want you fellows to spend a lifetime with me and be dependent on salary alone," he told them. "I hope we can build an equity in the company for you and your families so that you can look forward to retirement."

He continued the policy of bonuses throughout the late thirties and when stock in the company became publicly available after his wife Lillian Galvin died in 1942, he recommended that the bonuses be used for the purchase of stock. Galvin told each man that the bonus they received would vary according to their contributions to the company's effort. He advised them to buy stock in the company at the market price. And those employees who put their full bonus into stock would receive an added bonus in stock.

Some employees who bought and retained that early stock throughout the years of Motorola's phenomenal growth became wealthy, and a

few of them retired in their forties. Others, to
their everlasting regret, sold their stock at a profit
and then saw its sales value double and triple
many times in the years that followed.

It was understandable that not all of the employees would envision so vigorous a pattern of
growth and achievement. Some might even have
been eager to convert their stock into cash "before the company went under." A fortunate few
had Galvin's vision and assurance "that we will
make out all right in the end. It will be hard work
and a lot of disappointment but we will make out
all right."

In 1938 some of the first of the many Motorola employee organizations were formed. The
most important of all of these was the Service
Club which brought together the ten-year veter-
ans who had begun with Galvin in 1928. The first
Motorola Service Club party was held in 1939 in
Galvin's office and was attended by nine employees, three from 1928 and six from 1929. They
heard a warm and grateful tribute from Galvin
who was emotionally moved and from Joe who
was on the verge of tears.

In 1938, the Foremen's Club was organized,
and, in 1939, the Engineering Club held the first of
its monthly meetings devoted to educational talks
and demonstrations of technical advances. The
Credit Union was also formed in that year to
assist Motorolans in saving a part of their earn-

ings and to provide them the opportunity of borrowing money at a low rate of interest.

Galvin was not at first convinced of the need and effectiveness of employee organizations. In 1937, when a group of employees planned the first foremen's dance, Bill Arnos went to Galvin and offered him a number of complimentary tickets. Galvin asked, "What are we running a dance for?" When Arnos explained that it was for the purpose of morale, permitting the employees to see another side of each other then they displayed under the tensions of work, Galvin approved and called it a fine idea. Later, he came to champion his employee organizations and saw in them a way of building a company spirit. The Service Club remained closest to his heart, and these yearly banquets grew to incredible size and splendor as more employees achieved the ten-year mark which qualified them for membership.

It was true that Galvin felt there was no need for a union in his plant. He was not in sympathy with the function of unionism as a special interest against society. He did agree that in certain basic industries with a history of labor and management warfare, unions served a purpose. But he did not feel that his workers were either mistreated, underpaid, or abused. He did feel that there was a basic community of interest between them that should not be disturbed by an intermediary. They agreed with him and gave him a

moving loyalty which he returned with gratitude
and a loyalty of his own.

Infrequently, in later years, the company
would be pamphleteered. In response, the company
had to do no more than restate the values in the
growing list of Motorola benefits. In one early
episode, a group of handbill passing organizers
were driven off with blows by a group of factory
people. Galvin sternly reprimanded his people for
this violence assuring them there were other more
effective means of countering the organizers
based on a sound and progressive employee
program.

Only once, in the early 1950s, did the company have to resist a serious effort by a craft
union. So thoroughly did the employees support
the company that after some years of legal in-
volvement, the union withdrew its petition for an
election.

All of Galvin's feeling regarding the organization of his plant would probably have meant
little if the conditions under which his employees
worked were not the finest that his struggling
company could provide, and as his company pros-
pered, the finest possible. He gave them more
benefits and provided them better working conditions than a union might demand. He gave them
dignity and responsible participation within
the structure of their employment. He did these
things because he knew they were right, and like
the bread that was cast upon the waters, there

were obvious advantages in this practice for him. He had a greater freedom with his people, and could deal directly with each man in the way he thought best to serve the customer, the company, and its employees. He felt that serving the customer was, after all, the first and final justification for being in business. His people were tuned to this prime objective which made it possible for them to share in the rewards.

Perhaps to a greater extent than for many other founders of major American businesses, the company was Galvin's life. Its people were a part of his family, not in any benign paternalistic sense, but with a sincere recognition of their dignity as human beings. He could not be impersonal about the operation of the company, because it represented many things to him. It was his youth in Harvard with the popcorn stand. It was the move to Marshfield, Wisconsin with the battery company, full of anticipation, and the dismal retreat from there after failure. It was the excitement of the trip with Lillian and Bob to Atlantic City, and the months of trial and error to clear the endless bugs from car radio installations. It was the countless one-day stops to talk to dealers and service station operators. It was the core of his life—in myriad ways reflecting the many joys and satisfactions he had felt and sorrows he had endured.

He understood that his employees could not be expected to feel about the company as he felt.

He unquestionably saw his generous bonuses as a
partial solution to the problem of stimulating
energy and devotion to the company. But he
wasn't completely happy about any devotion
bought by gifts of money alone, regardless of how
he stressed, "These are given because they have
been earned." He was keenly aware of how difficult it was to produce loyalty in any individual.
Galvin had to convince his people of his genuine
interest, the sincerity of his feeling "that a company is only as effective as the people who staff it,
otherwise it is only four walls." That he succeeded against the numerous obstacles was evidenced by the respect and affection his people held
for him. Without this nucleus of loyalty built
through those first trying and tenuous years, the
company would not have been able to meet the
great challenge and demand of the Second World
War.

Diversification—
a Shaky Step
12

By 1936, the Galvin Manufacturing Corporation had exceeded the capacity of the building on Harrison Street and had spilled its facilities over into the Cracker Jack candy company building across the street. In the euphoria of the moment, it appeared that the hard and hazardous years were behind them. With his vision intent upon the future, Galvin decided to build a new office and factory to house the growing organization. He sent Joe and Earl McGowan on an intense search for a suitable parcel of land. Finally, a tract was selected and bought on Augusta Blvd., a few blocks east of Cicero Avenue. Impressed by the modern design of the buildings in the 1933 Century of Progress in Chicago, Galvin had the plans for the new building drawn along this line.

This expansion was a bold venture for the young company. The depression had battered the radio industry. A number of pioneer companies went bankrupt. As competition sharpened even more, the average price of sets was driven down with the majority of sales being small radio table models. A result of sharply reduced profit margins was that attention was primarily focused on cutting all possible corners, making "gimmick" improvements that had little effect upon the quality of the set, and undertaking few basic engineering changes. This was the corrosive effect of the depression in which engineering initiative was generally confined to small teams on a limited budget.

125

Under such conditions, any expansion was a hazardous undertaking, although Motorola had come a long way from the tenuous days when they depended for survival upon the repairing and making of the A and B Battery Eliminators.

On the twentieth of January, 1937, President Franklin D. Roosevelt delivered his second inaugural address in which he reemphasized his objectives of social justice. The challenge to American democracy, he said, is the "tens of millions of its citizens ... who at this very moment are denied the greater part of what the very lowest standards of today call the necessities of life ... I see one-third of a nation ill-housed, ill-clad, ill-nourished."

There were many portions of Roosevelt's New Deal that Galvin bitterly opposed, and, on a few occasions, he had written a letter to the President, "As a private citizen to tell him what I think." But he also had a moral sensitivity to the problems of the depression and its results in tragic human experience. In his earlier travels around the country selling car radio, he had been witness to the great human distress. He was in sympathy with government's aims to improve the standard of living. He had no sympathy with the old-fashioned, money-grasping philosophy of some of the industrial titans at the turn of the century.

As one of what he felt to be a new breed of American businessman, he felt there need be no discrepancy between business methods and principles and the national welfare. He saw business as a way of life and not merely a way of making money. And he felt that businessmen should not merely play Cassandras to the crisis, but initiate some active expansion of their own.

"Build for increased employment and expanded production," he told a group of businessmen at a luncheon. "Gamble that the country is sound and that we will make out all right." To prove he meant what he said, he ordered ground broken for the new Motorola plant.

"Well, P.V.," an associate of Galvin's told him brusquely, "you are barely out of the soup and you throw yourself back in again, hocked up to the gills."

Galvin coolly answered all the warnings by planning an elaborate house-warming banquet in the new cafeteria on the occasion of the completion of the new plant, a celebration for his employees and their families. He even brought in an orchestra to help make his point. This opening in April, 1937, was attended by almost one thousand employees and visitors.

Galvin's optimistic expectations seemed to be justified when contrary to all the predictions of disaster, additional production space was needed before they had fully moved into the new plant. He zestfully ordered the building of the Augusta annex.

Coincident with the opening of the Augusta

plant, Galvin had one of his hunches, often cannily accurate, but occasionally wrong. He felt that the time was ripe for the company to enter the home radio market more fully than their attempt in 1930 and 1931. For some time, his distributors had been urging him to design and manufacture a home-set line they could offer to their car-radio customers. The car radio was a seasonal business with heavy production scheduled for the first six months of the year. By the end of June, it was necessary to close down many of the lines and lay off a good number of the employees. Galvin thought of using home sets to cushion the period of each year from June through December.

Although in the early 1930s the company had produced some private brand home radios for manufacturers to install in their own cabinets, these were built to the manufacturers' specifications. By the spring of 1937, Galvin was thinking in terms of designing sets that would incorporate some of the innovations they had developed in car radio. He set a new group of his engineers to work on a rapid program to develop a complete line of table models, consoles, and phonographs at a laboratory in Forest Park, a suburb of Chicago, even before the Augusta Plant was finished.

One of the promised innovations of radio that year was push-button tuning. The problem involved was to set a button at each of the five to twenty required points or channels across the AM band. Since there were 108 AM channels across the country it was not feasible to have a set with a hundred push buttons but to settle upon a limited number of buttons, and then adjust the tuner to the desired local stations in the full range of the 108 channels. The problem was a difficult one that radio manufacturers grappled with earnestly.

Galvin introduced his new line at the Home Set Radio Convention in the summer of 1937. The distributors had enjoyed a record six months in car radio sales and came full of enthusiasm. They were delighted with the appearance of the new line and ordered in sizeable quantities. The Motorola shipping facilities went on a twenty-four hour schedule to rush the sets into the field.

It was not long, however, before distressing reports began to come back. The push buttons would simply not tune to the required stations. In addition, there were other complaints with tone, transformers and poor-quality parts failures.

In striving for innovation, the new home-radio engineers at Motorola had overlooked certain obvious factors. The push-button tuning did not work, and other start-up difficulties took the bloom off the dealer's initial enthusiasm.

But an even more serious national development was taking place. Precariously caught between the stagnation of the depression and Roosevelt's attempt to press his social and economic legislation, the country slid into a general business downturn in late 1937.

In addition to the political signs and general
economic portents, a scattered rash of price cutting with other lines at what should have been the
strong selling season made Galvin uneasy.

Experience had made him acutely sensitive to
the first signs of such a slide. In 1932, reading the
portents accurately, he had withdrawn the company's cash from the bank a week before it closed.
That modest cash reserve was all that stood between the company's continuing operation and instant insolvency. Once again he had a premonition
of what might happen, and acted just in time.

He made up his mind promptly to slash his
inventory. Wires were dispatched to the distributors inviting them to his office in small groups for
a series of meetings. There the order was given,
"Move on your inventory now, fast and hard."
Most distributors were at first incredulous, but
Galvin would not be second-guessed. "The storm
is coming," he told them. "Modest price reductions now will save us from major liquidations
sixty or ninety days from now."

Most of the distributors moved as he directed
and were able to avoid the frenzied dumping of
inventories as the situation became worse.

From sales of a little over seven million dollars in 1937, most of this realized through car
radio in the first six months of the year, Motorola's sales in 1938 fell to four and a half million
dollars. Almost two-thirds of the thousand
Motorola employees had to be laid off and the re-

maining people cut to three working days a week.

An indication of the hazardous economic condition of the company was reflected in a memo issued December 27, 1937, by Joe Galvin, stating, "Any articles to be purchased for any department costing more than $10 must be approved by Joe or Paul Galvin."

Galvin, in order to dramatize the urgent need for economy, dispensed with his secretary and for a period of months gave whatever letters he could not avoid answering to his bookkeeper to type, and he answered the phone himself.

But the successful push-button design for home and auto radio was to take some months of hard work, and, in the interim period, it was questionable whether Motorola could hang on. Here again, a fortuitous chain of circumstances evolved that permitted the company to weather the recession. The Philco Company in Philadelphia was hit by a severe strike that completely closed down its production facilities.

Although the radio industry was vigorously competitive, the managements of the principle companies were well acquainted with each other through personal contact and through their active and aggressive trade group, the Radio Manufacturers Association, which was formed in Chicago in 1924.

Galvin had made many friendships with other members of the association while working on industry problems, and these friendships included

some of the top management of Philco in a relationship of mutual respect.

Motorola became one of two companies selected in Chicago to produce some thousands of
Philco sets on a cost-plus basis. A group of Philco
engineers moved into the Augusta plant to work
closely with Motorola engineers and factory personnel.

Philco wanted a large quantity of home radio
sets produced in the shortest possible period of
time. Galvin preferred a more level labor load
hoping to sustain their lines until the seasonal increase in orders for car radio. Galvin was grateful for the production assignment and yet feared
that the period of full production would end all at
once and be followed by an interval of famine
from which they might not recover.

Fortunately for Motorola the Philco schedule
lasted until late in 1938 and by that time the brunt
of the recession had passed.

*   *   *   *

It was true that Galvin had been chastened by
the perilous year that he had barely survived.
After years of struggle, he had built the Augusta
plant thinking the worst of the turmoil was behind
him, believing that although the business required
constant attention, direction, and work, there
would never again be a question of actual survival.

Yet, he did not regret the experience. It became part of the large storehouse of victories and

defeats and near-disasters that he had experienced. He was never relentlessly optimistic, but fiercely determined to make things work. The recession in 1937–38 that caught him in the act of diversification into new products provided some sober reappraisals which he applied to other problems in later years. "I made the right move then," he would say wryly, "but it almost turned out to be the wrong time."

He might have relieved his situation slightly by vastly extending his degree of indebtedness but he had an abhorrence of debt. Even in later years, when the further expansion of the company required sizeable reserves of credit, he never became comfortably convinced that debt was desirable. When his accountants tried to convince him that debt was a relative matter, that large debt was disproportionate, but reasonable debt in relation to the size and potential of the company was something else, he answered, "You fellows have never been broke and never had the problem I've had.

"One Saturday night in 1930 I got home and before I had my coat and hat off, my wife Lillian, who had the rent to pay and food to buy, asked me, 'How much did you bring?' And I said, 'I brought 24 bucks,' and that's all they could give me—all the company could spare was 24 bucks. Now debt can smother a man and give him a false feeling of security when the truth is that even the 24 bucks he brings home might not really be his."

This evaluation was related to the way he regarded profit. He believed it was necessary for a man or a business to make a profit in order to get some satisfaction out of the effort. He believed in figuring the profit into a product or a venture at the beginning and holding to it at the marketplace. He believed, finally, that profit was a means to achieve everything else. The relatively modest way he always lived belied any personal adulation of money used unproductively or diverted to lavish self-indulgence.

It is doubtful whether even in his wildest dreams in those early days Galvin could have visualized the future of Motorola. He was not overly ambitious for great size or power. He had a love of building and would probably have been content as an architect or a builder. But he was also willing to establish limits to his horizons. He felt that to continue to build a certain number of good quality radio sets and make a fair profit was all he desired. When they were producing one hundred sets a day he would say, "Now this is about where we can stop."

When, by 1936, a year that saw almost a million and a half auto radios sold by the automobile and radio industry, as compared with 143,000 sold in 1932, and a year in which Galvin produced a much greater quantity of sets than he ever had before, he felt they were near their maximum. But obviously by this time a momentum had been built up and he began to visualize a favorable pattern of development. He understood the truth of the fundamental business axiom that a company either moved forward or backward ... there was no standing still.

He bound his company's destiny to this truth by saying, "We are moving forward!"

The Talkies—
Handie and Walkie
13

In 1936, the Galvin family took a six weeks tour of Europe. They sailed on the Italian liner, *Rex,* via the southern route to Italy. The trip was Galvin's first return to Europe since the war and he took a great pleasure in sharing the new experience with Lillian and thirteen-year-old Bob. He particularly enjoyed the tour of art galleries in Florence and later toured Austria, Germany, France, and England.

He came back from his visit to Germany convinced the situation was grave, and that war, unless a miracle intervened, was inevitable. His impressions of the almost frantic and unreasonable militancy among some of the German industrialists, the number of people in uniforms, and the other evident military preparations, suggested to him that the only possible outlet would be war. His impressions of the Autobahns, those great gleaming superhighways that criss-crossed Germany were, "They have not been built just for autos, they are war roads."

When he returned to the United States, through the expansion of early 1937 and the recession that ran into 1938, it was Galvin's feeling that the company should be working in product areas that might be useful to the country in case of war. He had a number of his engineers investigating applications of radio to the needs of the military.

But the real impetus for the beginning of Motorola's great war contributions came in early

1940 when Royal Munger, then financial editor for the *Chicago Daily News*, who was a reserve army officer, called Galvin. He told him that the National Guard then maneuvering in war games at Camp McCoy, Wisconsin were hampered for lack of radio communications.

Galvin sent Don Mitchell, his chief engineer, and Ray Yoder to Camp McCoy. During the inspection, Mitchell saw the heavy and cumbersome back-pack radios the Army was using for communications. "That's no kind of equipment with which to fight a war," Mitchell told Col. Leland H. Stanford of the U. S. Army Signal Corps. "I think we can provide better radios for that purpose."

Col. Stanford took Mitchell up on his confident assertions. Mitchell returned to Galvin and spoke of his feeling that a light and portable transceiver could be built.

Without any specific contract from the Army, Galvin urged Mitchell to go all out in developing such a unit. Mitchell, with Ray Yoder, Jack Davis, Paul Smith, and several other Motorola engineers assisting them, set to work.

The problems inherent in any portable unit of this kind were enormous, the paramount one being that of weight. The army requirements were that the unit be made of the lightest possible material known, in this instance, magnesium. Mitchell, knowing that magnesium was relatively new and that there would be all kinds of difficulty in appli-

cation, worked on the problem of designing the
unit in such a way that the more familiar alumi-
num could be used, and still remain within the
Army's weight restriction.

Another problem was that in actual combat
enemy snipers could locate the radio—by the reflection of the antenna. The task became one of
finding a black corrosion resistant, non-reflective
nickel plating for the antenna. There was plenty
of black plating, but since the antenna would have
to be retractable, the constant friction would
scratch and nick it and reimpose the reflective
properties on any coating then known. A coating
was finally developed by one of Motorola's engineers which would resist the abrasion.

There were numerous working models that
failed to meet specification in one way or another.
But with the brilliant engineering teamwork under
the direction of Don Mitchell evidencing the same
zestful group spirit that had successfully whipped
the earlier problem of the car radio, a working
model was produced. This prototype was the
famous "Handie-Talkie" radio, a two-way crys-
tal-controlled portable radio no larger than a
cracker box, complete with a microphone, head-
antenna and self-contained batteries. It was built
with the precision of a pocket calculator and
weighed slightly more than five pounds. It had a
solid range of one mile and a potential range of up
to three miles.

After three months, and with three sets to

demonstrate, Mitchell flew to Ft. Benning, Georgia, where maneuvers were then in progress, to show them to the Army. Although individual officers, such as Col. Stanford, were tremendously enthusiastic, there was apprehension in higher military echelons about the effectiveness of these small frail looking units in actual combat. A small quantity of them were finally contracted for.

Galvin was disappointed at the initial lack of response to what he knew was an amazing unit. Mitchell and Yoder continued to work on the product seeking ways to improve it.

The "Handie-Talkie" radio was given a sharp impetus, when, during his inauguration in 1940, President Roosevelt saw some of the units being used for purposes of security by the police and the secret service. He wrote a letter concerning them to the military officials involved at that time in organizing the paratroopers, and once more Galvin arranged a field demonstration. This time the validity and uniqueness of the product was instantly recognized and Motorola received some major contracts for their immediate production and delivery. The company went into full production in July of 1941, six months before Pearl Harbor.

The "Handie-Talkie" two-way radio, or SCR-536, the Signal Corps number for the unit, saw action in every theatre of war in the world during the next five years, with nearly 40,000 of these units being made for the various services.

To manufacture this quantity at that time—the production on a mass basis of a complete transmiting and receiving station in one tiny unit composed of 585 miniature sized parts with its own power supply—was a miracle of modern electronic engineering. They went into service at the very beginning of combat with ground forces and Air Force gliders, becoming for the infantryman a piece of equipment second only to his rifle in importance. It was in the North African invasion, where communications inadequacies were crucial, that they proved their essential worth.

Besides being used by front line troops for reporting positions, locations of machine gun nests, shell fire, mortar batteries and to call for air support and supplies, the "Handie-Talkie" radio was used by airborne troops and paratroopers. Each set was completely waterproofed and could be submerged in water without losing its operating efficiency.

At one point in the war, Motorola received an order for 100 of these units to be delivered to a point of embarkation within two days for a "special and most urgent emergency." The order had not been received through Army channels and, seeking confirmation, Galvin was unable to establish the point of origin. Going on a hunch, however, he had the Signal Corps label cut off of 100 units and had them sprayed a dull gray instead of the usual olive-drab and shipped them to arrive in time at the point of embarkation. He did not find out until many months later that the group that received them were the famous "Carlson's Raiders."

Although Motorola was to produce a wide and diversified array of products for the armed services during the war, the "Handie-Talkie" radio and the later Walkie-Talkie played primary roles in earning the company five Army-Navy "E" Awards. As a mark of esteem for his part in designing and developing the "Handie-Talkie" radio the *Chicago Tribune* on September 21, 1944 presented Don Mitchell with their War Worker's Award, and later he received a special citation from the Army as well.

* * * *

During the early 1930s, a few police departments and engineers dabbled in rigging up radio communications for police cars. For a short time, one of the Chicago broadcast stations would interrupt a soap opera to send an emergency message to police that kept their car radios tuned to that station. The radio public had the enjoyment and vicarious thrill of listening in on this additional drama, but unfortunately the Chicago criminals took up monitoring the station as well and timed their getaway to the radio alert.

As early as 1931, Motorola engineers modified the coils of standard auto radio sets, which permitted the radios to receive the reassigned higher frequency police signals above the broadcast band. This frequency change somewhat im-

proved the one-way police communications, but
the results were still only marginally effective because the criminals had their sets adapted also.

These early experiences clearly revealed that
police departments could use and would use radio
receivers and transmitters in quantity and with
striking effectiveness if a way could be found to
solve the inherent design and use problems.

This was evident to a number of people.
Galvin started to do something about it in a serious way because, as he said, "There was a need
and I could see it was a market that nobody
owned."

By 1939, men like Elmer Wavering, Art
Reese, Floyd McCall, Dave Chapman, Harry Harrison, and Herby Moos were concentrating on the
technical, production, and selling problems of police radio.

The new department, which they expanded
with ability and vigor, didn't even have a formal
name. It was called simply the "Herby Moos Spe-
cialty Department" after Moos who ran the factory part of the operation. This small group was
the highly personalized nucleus of what was to be
called the Police Radio Department, and eventually the Communications Division of the company.

In early 1940, Galvin read in a technical jour-
nal of the work of a professor at the University of
Connecticut, Daniel Noble, who had developed an
FM mobile communications system for the Con-

necticut State Police. Dan Noble was the first man to establish an FM system to the specialized requirements of a police department. He had designed and supervised the building of an FM broadcast system for WRDC, of Hartford, Connecticut, and he had served as consultant for similar projects.

Galvin was greatly impressed with Noble's achievements and established contact with him to arrange a series of meetings. He found Noble lukewarm about any permanent move from the academic world to industry. A final agreement between the two men encompassed a trial period, whereby Noble would take a year's leave of absence from the University and join Motorola.

In the beginning Noble was regarded by a few Motorola employees as primarily a visionary, an academician, impatient with price and profit considerations and with anything that restricted his pure research. His appearance, a tall, contemplative big man with big strong hands, an imposing bow tie and tufts of frizzled hair gilding a high and lustrous bald head, suggested the universal image of the "egg head," the dreamer who could not be depended upon to keep his feet solidly on the ground.

A part of the problem was simply that Motorola achievements in the early days had been effected by unorthodox engineering talent, by men without academic degrees, but with a canny facility in terms of screwdrivers and soldering irons. Some of these men looked upon Noble as an intruder.

Galvin came to admire the brilliant vision of Noble, and came to place great faith and trust in that vision. Noble came to respect and care greatly for the silver-haired man who stood only a shade above his shoulder, who could not move glibly in any involved discussion of physics, but who had a remarkable capacity to cut through a maze of issues, even technical ones, and touch the pertinent core. There was a period perhaps when they tested one another, and with the mutual respect this produced, they became a formidable combination.

Noble joined the company in early September 1940. He began by working on the possibility of adapting many of the AM systems common in that time to FM. He had no responsibility in the development of the "Handie-Talkie" radio but went to Fort Monmouth, New Jersey, with Don Mitchell to make the presentation of the unit to the Signal Corps. Among the Signal Corps officers present at that time were two, Col. Colton, and Major J. D. O'Connell, who would play important roles in the development of a longer range portable unit than the "Handie-Talkie" radio.

Sometime after the United States had gone to war, on a visit to Washington, Noble was told by Col. O'Connell that the Signal Corps had let a contract for the development of a new AM portable transmitter-receiver. Noble told him bluntly that he felt this was a grave mistake, and that the area of development should be for an FM portable unit. Noble felt strongly such a unit could be developed and that Motorola could do it. As a result of this conversation, and Noble's confidence in the company's ability to meet the challenge, Col. O'Connell issued a Signal Corps contract for the development of an FM portable transmitter-receiver to Motorola.

A series of meetings were held with Signal Corps Engineers at Fort Monmouth, and engineering meetings at Motorola were attended by Noble's team, which included Henry Magnuski, Marion Bond, Lloyd Morris, and Bill Vogel. Working furiously against time, this brilliant team developed a design which included a single tuning control to tune both the transmitter and the receiver simultaneously and an automatic frequency control to insure clear communication without the need for critical precision tuning on the part of the operator. They also overcame the primary problems of establishing an adequate power supply, a minimum number of crystals, and the fungiciding of the unit to allow it to withstand tropical temperatures and humidity.

The final critical acceptance test took place at Fort Knox, Kentucky, where Col. O'Connell had set up a conference for the testing of a variety of portable and mobile communications equipment. Members of the Infantry Board, always highly

critical of the application of communications
equipment to battlefield conditions, had been invited as observers. Bob Galvin accompanied Dan
Noble and Bill Vogel to Fort Knox for these crucial tests. Since they only had two working models,
each night was spent in the hotel checking them
over carefully to make sure they were ready for
additional tests the following day. The performance of the SCR-300, Walkie-Talkie, during
those tests, its capacity to communicate through
interfering ignition noise, and the rugged quality
of the design, met with unusually enthusiastic
response from the hard-headed Infantry and
Signal Corps officers.

Motorola was to produce nearly 50,000 of
these famed SCR-300 Walkie-Talkie units during
the course of the war, the first units transported
by air for use in the invasion of Italy by the Allied
Forces. A sizeable quantity went to the Pacific.
Perhaps their greatest contribution was in the
European invasion, where their role in re-establish-
ing order at the conclusion of the Battle of the
Bulge gained Motorola tremendous recognition
and a general feeling that perhaps the Walkie-
Talkie was the single most useful piece of communications equipment employed in the invasion.

Noble was awarded a Certificate of Merit
from the Army for his part in the development of
the Walkie-Talkie. Noble, accepting the award,
stressed the major contributions of Magnuski,
Vogel, Morris and Bond. He went on to say that

the development of the Walkie-Talkie was an academic exercise compared to the contribution of the men on the battlefields, the men fighting the war.

Noble's decision in 1941 not to return to the University of Connecticut came about because he knew he could be of greater help to the war effort with Motorola. There were also long discussions with Galvin pressing him on the challenges of industry's work in the private enterprise system, the complex problems involved in taking the product of creative inventiveness and harnessing it to the needs of customers. Noble grew to recognize the validity of these challenges.

At the end of the war, Noble turned the major part of his attention to the growth of the mobile communications business. He was able, with the help of an extraordinary team of Motorola engineers, along with Art Reese, Homer Marrs, and Floyd McCall on the marketing phase, to establish the Motorola product as the best in the country. From this foundation, the communications division grew to a position of undisputed leadership in the field of mobile and portable two-way communications.

In 1948, he urged Galvin into the opening of a small research facility in Phoenix, Arizona for the purpose of exploring new skills and opportunities in the rapidly advancing art of military electronics. Both men wished to continue making contributions to the country's military potential, and both men were convinced that it was logical to set up an operation away from the bomb-vulnerable major urban centers.

But equally important was Noble's feeling, discussed many times with Galvin, that the electronic art was headed for a major change, one characterized by the rising importance of solid state electronics. The new pattern would require synthesizing the skills of many separate disciplines, mathematicians, physicists, metallurgists and chemists working with electronic engineers, all moving together toward rising scientific sophistication in the electronics art as a whole.

There were a few conservative voices at Motorola in 1948 who felt there wasn't anything Noble wanted to do in Phoenix that couldn't be done just as well at headquarters. There were references to the Phoenix venture as "Noble's Yacht" and "Noble's Folly." Galvin himself may have had a few reservations, but he had been a witness through the years of the war to the many contributions that Noble made with two-way radio and military electronics, and he backed him firmly, telling the objectors, "You don't argue with success."

The first military electronics laboratory was set up in Phoenix in January of 1949, and made an important contribution to the efforts of American industry in the Korean War. Following the war, Noble hired Dr. William Taylor as his first solid state, or semiconductor, scientist. Dr. Taylor invented the processing procedure which produced practical large-area junctions and established Motorola as the first producer of power transistors.

The military electronics division operation matured rapidly after Joe Chambers became general manager, and this division served as the birthplace of the semiconductor products division and the solid state systems division.

Certainly one of the reasons for the establishment of the first facility at Phoenix was that it was a clean city, with good schools, and an intellectual aura of growth and progress. There was also the Arizona climate as a great drawing card in the recruitment of the best qualified engineers and scientists with their families. But more basic was the principle fact that Noble anticipated the trend toward solid state electronics, and wanted to help to mold the trend in a creative sense.

Perhaps, like Plato in the Hellas of antiquity who dreamed of establishing an ideal society, Noble also conceived of a group of engineers and scientists in an operation so organized and administered that each man could achieve a high level of personal identification and dedication by being given the right to accept the responsibility for the ultimate success or failure of his contribution. This could be achieved in the development of an operation that would combine the virtues of the men of "ideas" with the virtues of the men who could adapt these ideas. In that way, there would be created a new exemplary path from idea to engineering, from engineering to production, and finally to the product in the hands of the customer.

"Big game" sales convention head table with "Vic" Irvine,
Walt Stellner, Joe Galvin, Paul Galvin,
Elmer Wavering, and Allan Williams

Judging a pie-eating contest at company outing

Motorola goes to war with the "Handie-Talkie"

. . . and also with the famed Walkie-Talkie

Army Certificate of Merit
was presented to Daniel E. Noble, center,
for his work on the Walkie-Talkie.
Motorola received the
Army-Navy E Award five times

War Department
citation in 1946
for patriotic service

Cutting the birthday
cake at a gala
old-timers' dinner

Visitors often found Paul Galvin in his shirtsleeves

"Be Calm, Use Foresight, and Pray"
14

As the years of the Second World War were a time of great crises for the nation, in a subordinate sense they were also a time of stress and achievement for Galvin. He had survived a decade and a half of struggle and near-disaster guiding his small company to some measure of security. In his middle forties he was the tough and resolute product of his past, energetic and determined, a canny salesman and splendid administrator, and a visionary with his feet planted solidly on the ground. He had a genuine humility and a sense of humor which let him see his own sometimes frantic gyrations in proper perspective. He placed the same vigorous emphasis on courage and common sense that Theodore Roosevelt did.

Most important of all, for the responsibility which lay ahead for him, Galvin had a love for and a faith in the industry of which he was only a tiny part. It came, therefore, as no surprise to those who knew him well when the Radio Manufacturers Association elected him president, a position he was to hold during the crucial years of the war. It is particularly significant since the association included most of the giant radio corporations with very capable and, in many cases, better known leaders.

Galvin had always felt that the American radio industry was a striking example of a private enterprise system at work. Its people had no monopolistic cartel umbrella comfortably protecting their activities. They had large and small com-

panies competing for the same market—the little
fellow many times licking the big fellow to a
standstill. They had efficient mass production, a
great variety of specialists, and superb engineers.
They had a proven relationship with scores of
component manufacturers. Though they had always lived in an atmosphere of stiff competition,
when genuine and proper cooperation was in
order for the benefit of the public and the industry, they could always get together.

Galvin accepted the RMA presidency feeling
that the radio industry would do its part in the
war and after. To those prophets of gloom and
despair who envisaged the collapse of their normal markets, he said, "Problems are not new to
us in this industry. We have always had them and
we will always have them. Great or small they
must be answered; maybe not to our entire satisfaction but somehow answered. Let us keep our
mental feet on the ground, be calm, use foresight, and pray for the day when this too shall
pass."

With the advent of the war in December of
1941, Galvin's marked ability to act as a catalyst
between opposing factions stood him in good
order in the organizing of various RMA commit-
tees.

"You couldn't sit in the room with the man
and be petty," one of his competitor associates of
those years said. "He had a way of deprecating

the little rivalries and jealousies and making you see they were not really important.''

When the government began to impose rigorous controls and restrictions, Galvin opposed those association members who advocated heated protest by saying, ''We must reconcile ourselves to the fact that we must park our heritage of private enterprise; at least until the end of the war and let us hope no longer.''

While he soberly tried to answer a reasonable grievance, he had little patience with selfish men who could not see beyond their own immediate interest. Once during a meeting, when an affluent vice-president of another firm vehemently protested what he felt was an inadequate profit margin on one of his products, Galvin flared, ''Don't you understand that men who make less in a year than you make in a week are dying while you carp about profits?''

As president of the RMA, Galvin was directly involved with all phases of the problems concerning wages, manpower, industry capacity, materials shortages, and allocation of strategic materials. There were numerous trips to Washington to plead for scarce metals with which to do their job. He had his own moments of sharp discouragement. ''This might be a wild prediction,'' he told a meeting of the Priorities Committee, ''but I think the priorities thing will become so involved that, as far as we are concerned, we may all be on a committee in Washington this time next year.''

The whole business as he pungently summed it up was a far cry from the old days when "You either made radios or you didn't.''

He fought also what he felt were the discriminatory priorities rating of some other industries over the radio industry. In a speech of June, 1941 he said, "Radio is not a luxury like a lot of home appliances. It is downright essential to public security. It's our job to convince these fellows in these bureaus in Washington who are dividing the peanuts that the radio industry is essential to public security and national defense.''

He was determined to set an untarnished example in the way his own company met its wartime responsibilities. He succeeded so well that at one point during the war General William Harrison of the Signal Corps suggested to the heads of a number of large corporations that they visit Motorola for an example of speed and competence in research and production and for the marvelous "esprit de corps'' that characterized the working relationships of its people.

It was true that although Motorola was certainly not the largest prime contractor serving the Army, there were few other companies large or small which could point to a more enviable record in engineering accomplishment, service, delivery, and quality of product.

An example of this position in the industry came about in the case of quartz crystals. Each radio receiver and transmitter used in the communications systems of the military required quartz crystals to hold their many signal frequencies constant. An average of about 80 crystals per set, with as many as 120 crystals in a single set. With the rapidly expanding military requirements for communications equipment, a real crystal procurement problem peaked in the early part of 1942. Prior to that time, the crystal industry nationally had a total production of between 50,000 and 75,000 crystals a year.

In the autumn of 1941, the crystal requirement appeared to be no more than about 600,000 to 750,000. By the end of the first sixty days of 1942, it became evident that the crystal program would have to deliver between three and three-and-a-half million crystals. Since there was no way the existing facilities could produce such quantities, a crystal industry had to be developed almost overnight.

Galvin assigned Elmer Wavering to take charge of this crystal program, and Wavering performed a series of real miracles in developing an adequate number of qualified suppliers. Numerous loft operations were set up to produce crystals. These small producers required a definite organization to direct the procurement of materials, engineering, and production; Wavering directed this task from finding people to be trained, locating supply sources, getting the crystals made, and arranging for delivery.

By December of 1942, under Wavering's
fruitful guidance, aided by Frank Brewster who
became chief crystal engineer, there were between
thirty and thirty-five crystal manufacturers established. The great majority of them had never seen
a crystal six months before. By December, 1942,
they were delivering crystals through Motorola at
the rate of 125,000 to 150,000 a week and by
March, 1943, they had upped this quantity to between 200,000 and 250,000 per week. By the end of
the war, Motorola delivered almost 35 million
crystals, more than half of all the crystals used in
the entire war effort.

Immensely conscious of the important role
radio was playing in the war, Galvin prodded his
associates into a recognition of their awesome responsibility.

"I wonder how many of you realize the importance radio is playing as a major deciding
factor in who is going to win the war? What is
it that gives the vicious efficiency to vehicles of
destruction in modern mechanized warfare? It is
radio. What is it that is today revolutionizing
aircraft, naval and anti-aircraft tactics and
strategy? It is radio and radar. It is our job—the
industry's job—to deliver these precious and important instruments."

Galvin could not possibly fulfill his obligations on an industry level and still effectively concentrate on the running of his own business. Much
of this added company burden fell on Joe's shoul-

ders, and he drove himself to the point of exhaustion in meeting the challenge. He was aided by the tight and efficient organization team Galvin and he had built through the thirties.

As in the case of almost all of the firms in essential industries, by May, 1942, the war effort completely dominated Motorola's production. In addition to the "Handie-Talkie" radio and the Walkie-Talkie, the company produced synchroscopes, marker beacons, radar search equipment, automatic tracking airborne range equipment, portable vehicular transmitter-receivers, and radar beacons.

In addition to this production, and on its own initiative, Motorola continued to allocate a small portion of its facilities to the production of two-way communications equipment for the various local, state, and federal agencies in the United States. Galvin believed that his company had an obligation to continue to supply these instruments of internal security. The War Production Board agreed. During most of the war, only two other companies also manufactured small quantities of such equipment, but during the period of the WPB Motorola supplied 85 per cent of all such two-way mobile communications equipment.

Another singular achievement of this period was Galvin's success in assisting his consumer product wholesale distributors to remain in business at a time when so many similar concerns were failing. He did this as much out of friendship for

the individuals involved as he did for the reason
that it was good business. He felt that his close
friendship with men like Nate Cooper and Frank
Kearns and "Dutch" Moore and all the rest, as
well as the fine organization they had welded
together, were his real wealth.

In May, 1942, when the government ordered
a complete ban on production of new cars and
radios for civilian use, Motorola had in the vi-
cinity of 125,000 brand new car radios in inventory and no new automobiles were being produced
to absorb them. This was the situation when
Galvin confronted the national convention of his
distributors that year. The problem was simply
how to keep his whole distributor organization
from folding up because of lack of anything to
sell.

He met the problem first by a canny program
to salvage the car radios. With all new car production stopped there was no car market for the
radios but there were no restrictions on selling
existing home radios to consumers. Led by Elmer
Wavering and the resourceful Detroit distributor
Lewis Ingram, the company engineers managed to
convert these 125,000 six-volt battery units into
home radios capable of working on 110-volt house
current. Because wood was not classified as a
strategic material, they managed to get cabinets
built. When these hybrid sets were finally completed, they were the only new home radios
available in the country.

These sets became a saving grace for many Motorola distributors, providing them a product to sell through the first months of transition from a peacetime to a wartime economy. By the time these sets had run out, Lew Ingram, joined by Vic Irvine, created an intricate subcontracting complex that provided the distributors a variety of items to make and sell including toys, paints, mirrors, play equipment, wall heaters, tables, coils, crystal holders, and even crystals. Lew Ingram supplied one distributor with sewing machines to set his people to finishing knapsacks and another handled a product which absorbed oil on the floors of factories and garages.

Nor did Galvin forget his and the industry's suppliers in this period. Limited only by his paramount wartime obligation to the military, he put the full facilities of his company at the suppliers' disposal, including engineering, and help in materials allocation.

By this foresight with both distributor and supplier principals, Galvin cemented what had been an already fine organization with an adhesive of added loyalty, a loyalty that would have important benefits for him when the war ended and the company moved into the competitive postwar market.

"Turning on a Dime"
15

As early as June of 1943, Galvin could say, addressing the RMA Convention in Chicago, "We must begin thinking of a transition back to a peacetime economy." At the same time he cautioned them about extravagant claims. "Some in our midst are playing a dangerous game of advocating fantastic designs and models. I don't know whether it's excess profits or the ants in the pants of some advertising men trying to keep busy while the boss is busy on war work."

He felt the accelerated war effort had taught the men of the radio industry many things they could not hope to crowd into the first models released immediately after the war. They were going to have to live on the application of these new discoveries to models they would release for a number of years. For that reason, he counseled that they be more realistic in their representations to the trade and to the public.

In June, 1944, Galvin began pressing for an orderly program to be worked out in conjunction with industry leaders and officials of the WPB. He felt it should be set forth just how the WPB Limitation Order would be altered after the German phase of the war had been concluded to permit industry re-entry into some civilian production while still continuing their military production for the Japanese war.

Anticipating the immensity of the move back into civilian production, Galvin felt that when the German phase of the war was successfully won, the military people would no longer need all of the facilities and workers of the industry for war work. When that time came, they should be fully prepared to turn quickly to some civilian production to keep their people working.

He knew that a serious cutback in military requirements would cause many plants to be closed down and a great number of employees to be laid off unless their engineering departments were ready with newly designed models to fill the gap. To achieve this aim he felt that merchandising plans should be prepared. The early development of such a program seemed to him not only important to the industry but important to the public.

Galvin knew that the industry would be faced with a tremendous backlog of consumer demand for radio which could keep their plants busy for years. In fact, the prospects of the radio industry looked so good, and the grass on their side of the fence so green, that he felt that people in other industrial areas, with excess production facilities would become interested in radio. His strong competitive feeling was to let them come, but he warned wryly, "I'm afraid that some people who will wander into our industry, looking for the fast and the easy buck, will learn by bitter experience that it is not the place for the faint-hearted."

Galvin reserved his most enthusiastic anticipation for television. He thought it reasonable that those in the radio manufacturing business should be the ones who would develop, produce and merchandise television sets. He knew there was a great variance of opinion as to just when and how television would take hold after the war and that there would be numerous problems in the matter of frequency allocations and systems standards.

Much of that anticipation would have to wait until the industry had fulfilled its obligations in concluding the war, but Galvin was not moderate in his pronouncements about the prospects. "When we do get post-war television," he said, "it will be the advent of a great business and we will have another industry as big or much bigger than the radio industry."

On the first of May, 1945, the provisional German government announced Adolph Hitler's death. The following day Berlin fell and the German forces in Italy surrendered. By the ninth of May, the German surrender was formally ratified at Berlin.

Although there were still some months of bloody fighting in the Pacific, the eventual outcome became clear.

Through the last eighteen months of the war, Motorola's military engineering effort had been shifted in primary emphasis from radio communications to radar. The refinement of the company's pre-war scientific principles and the development of new techniques like radar put Motorola in a sound technical position to enter the post-war market.

Meanwhile, there were the massive post-war readjustments and alterations to be made. As in the case with countless other firms, almost immediately after VJ-Day on September 2, 1945 Motorola received cancellations of war contracts aggregating approximately $34 million. By November 30, 1945, final delivery of all military equipment still to be shipped had been made.

The sales volume for the fiscal year ending November 30, 1945 was about $68 million compared with approximately $87 million the year before.

Faced with a similar situation, a number of companies began an earnest and rather desperate retrenchment by closing plants and cutting the wages of employees they retained. Galvin made Motorola's position on that point trenchant and clear.

"We all know wage rates and salaries have gone up during the war and there's a lot of talk about what should be done with these so-called higher war-wage rates. With us the problem is settled—we're not going to make any reductions in wage rates or salaries of any kind. We are convinced that with proper planning and proper cooperation between employees and management, these so-called wartime rates can continue to be paid on future civilian production. We

think it is important to our employees that this
issue be settled in their minds now and we propose
to tell them no wage reductions of any kind."

When he was told that some of his associates
in the industry disagreed with his ideas about the
immediate prospects, he replied, "The fact that
we disagree is good for the industry and good for
the country." When he was accused of unfounded
optimism, he answered, "Of course we can't hold
the war level—but we are not going back to where
we were before the war and this is only a beginning for what will be one of the greatest decades
in our century."

Galvin's ability to move boldly and quickly
was reflected in the profit and loss statement of
Motorola for 1946. The first six months of that
year, evidencing the difficult conversion from war
to a civilian economy, showed the company with a
loss of about $600,000. By the end of the year the
loss had not only been made up but a profit of
about $600,000 was earned. This profit was made
in a year when rival companies, large and small,
were showing severe losses. Galvin had always insisted that the company be able to "turn on a
dime" and 1946 proved it could.

Motorola came out of the war covered with
glory, but it was still a relatively small and
hungry company. Its image until the war had been
completely founded upon fine car radios, although
the company had also manufactured some home
sets. Now Galvin set his goal to enter the home

radio business in a much bigger way—to add phonograph products as well and to parlay the company's leadership in two-way radio communications into a secure and growing business.

With the filing of an application for listing an additional issue of Motorola stock on the New York Stock Exchange, Galvin was questioned closely by the president of the exchange and the members of the Stock List Committee on the prospects of television. Some of the members raised their eyebrows at what they thought was an overly enthusiastic evaluation of the potential market for that product. But Galvin knew, as did many other leaders in the radio industry, that the great post-war boom would be in television. And the funds to be raised by the new issue of stock would go to finance Motorola's entry into that field as well.

Galvin knew his only chance to compete with the larger companies was to enter the market with a really fine product. To be successful a television set had to be well engineered, easy to produce on an assembly line, and provide excellent performance. In addition, Galvin wanted a television set that would be bold and original in design and construction and that yet could be marketed at a price equal to or lower than the prices being charged for similar sets at that time.

In preparation for this aim, he had Dan Noble hire a group of talented engineers from M.I.T. Radiation Laboratory, among whom was

George Fyler, an engineer with considerable background in consumer electronics, and set them to work on a television research and development program. There was already another group of Motorola engineers who had experimental television receivers in operation before the war. In a rather novel approach Galvin set the two groups competing by having one group proceed along orthodox lines and the other group striking out in a new direction to work out a new design.

Galvin had begun setting up a post-war television "operational team" in March of 1946. He believed that by the time a set got into production it should already have been completely integrated into the other functions of the company—purchasing, sales, advertising and merchandising, and thoroughly field tested.

In addition to television, Galvin and Elmer Wavering were enthusiastic about another product design which the company had developed before and during the war and felt had a great potential. This was a gasoline burner automobile heater which they felt successfully met the problem of being thermostatically adjustable in the car by a pre-set control.

A great deal of time and effort and money went into this product which was heralded in the company's promotional literature as "sensational." It claimed outstanding features such as heat flowing in less than a minute, a constant heat control, and maintaining temperatures at 50, 60, 70, or 80 degrees by an automatic heat selector. As blithely confident as a skater skimming over a patch of ice he does not know is dangerously thin, Galvin affirmed, "All the prestige of Motorola is behind this great car heater."

The gasoline heater turned out to be a costly and unsalvageable mistake. It never continued to work correctly under actual operating field conditions, and one of the major difficulties, that of being able to find a method to properly exhaust the gasoline fumes, was never solved.

The heater project was dropped and buried in April, 1948, the sizeable losses unhappily absorbed, and although Galvin did not brood about mistakes, he was candid to admit, "When we make one, it's a whopper!"

In later years, when some of his people became especially enthused about a development which he supported with some reservation, Galvin would give them approval to push ahead while quietly warning, "Let's not have another heater situation."

He understood that the climate of innovation and zest in the company made such mistakes a possibility. From the days when he was employed at Brach Candy Company for Mr. Emil Brach, he estimated the real potential of a company could be gauged by the amount of obsolete machinery it amassed. He believed that a good part of the reason his own company had grown was because of the tenuous beginning, the uncertainty of their early days in radio.

"We had to learn all the way. We had no sponsorship, no money, no business. The car radio idea in 1930 was very unpopular from a conservative point of view. People said, 'Who wants a car radio? It will ruin your motor.' For this reason our business attracted very young men who hoped to grow up with a new industry and were willing to take a chance. The enthusiasm of these young men, plus our emphasis on sound engineering, made us grow. Sometimes, enthusiasm causes us to make a dandy mistake but without the enthusiasm we would never have survived anyway."

But if the gasoline heater was a disaster, the venture into television was a different story. The 10-inch set introduced by RCA became a standard for the industry. It was a fine design with large components, and conservatively specified circuits. It retailed for a price well over $300.

It was evident that RCA had set a successful product pattern for itself and that all other companies would follow that lead. If Motorola, a company that had been an also-ran in the home radio market, was to move to a position of prominence in the related field of television, then it would have to do something distinctive.

Each of the two competitive television engineering teams at that time under the direction of Home Products Vice President Walt Stellner, came up with excellent designs. One of them, in which Ray Yoder played a principal role, gave the company a product, the VT-101 which was at least equal to the RCA design. The other team, which had George Fyler as chief engineer, proposed a distinctive bold new approach which came to be known as the VT-71, the "golden view" of television for 1947.

The VT-71 was a superbly compact unit with a 7-inch screen. The set weighed 25 pounds and could easily be carried from room to room. It employed novel circuitry, the first inter-carrier sound, an electrostatic picture tube with advanced deflection circuits, a vastly improved high voltage supply, and an inexpensive switch type seven-channel tuner.

As this model started to take form in the laboratory, the product and market strategy took shape in Galvin's mind. He felt this set provided Motorola a real opportunity to market a superior product at a price well under the industry minimum.

It was at just such times as this—key potential turning points in the company's affairs—that Galvin would add the vital links to the Motorola strategies and plans. He recognized that for his distributors to be placed in a leading position in the TV race for the years to come, a fast break at the beginning would be required. Once every major company had established a position, it would take many more times the effort and investment to move up the ladder. Motorola's resources were still comparatively limited, so he did not relish a long expensive contest with the outcome in doubt.

He called his management together and announced that Motorola was going to sell 100,000 TV receivers in its first year. He didn't ask them if they could but told them bluntly they would. To some who sat in that meeting, the announcement bordered on madness. To others it was an electrifying dream that was questionable of attainment. As one of his associates reconstructed the discussion years later, the objections were many and heated.

"Our new 'T' plant hasn't nearly the capacity for that kind of production," one man said.

"A plant can always build more than you thought it could," Galvin answered. "Our plant will do it."

"We'll never sell that quantity," another man said. "That would make our industry position third or fourth, and the best we've ever been in home radio is seventh or eighth."

"We'll sell them," Galvin said, "because we've got a superior product and we're setting a price that will raise some thunder." He paused for dramatic effect. "That price will be $179.95 and with a good discount to our distributors."

"We're not even sure we can break $200 yet!" an engineer protested.

"That's the price," Galvin said bluntly. "I've got a hunch that's the price. I don't want to see any more cost sheets until you provide me a profit at that price and that volume. We'll work ourselves into it."

One of Galvin's special skills was an ability to see a whole situation and its consequences. Within the framework of this skill, he had an intuitive ability to set major achievable goals, achievable to him even though not always evident to others in the beginning.

The marketing plan for the VT-71 was similar to the time in 1934 when Galvin determined to market the Motorola car radio at $49.95. Though most of his people felt it couldn't be done, he knew his organization better than they knew themselves. "We'll work ourselves into a profit," he'd say. He somehow sensed the market at that time was ready for a car radio at $49.95. It might not have been ready the year before and the year after might have been too late.

There is indeed in business an art in recognizing the right time, being ready for it, and acting. This art of timing was Galvin's particular strength. Although hardly infallible, as he was the first to admit, the frequency with which he was right was astounding. The timing on the car radio was right and the timing on the VT-71 was right.

In the beginning the reaction to the VT-71 was one of astonishment and grudging admiration. Garth Heisig, one of the engineers on the project at that time, recollects taking one of the units into a dealer in Somerville, Mass. and demonstrating its quality. The dealer unhappily admitted that it worked fine but he "had just sold a competitive model priced at $650 and why should he push the Motorola model at $179.95?"

But that dealer's reaction was not general. A majority of them, stirred up as much by the first enthusiastic reports from customers as by the tub-thumping of the distributors, realized that the volume of sets they could sell would more than compensate for the higher profit on the more expensive sets. As the VT-71 began to catch on, it tore a wide place in the market and in a matter of months Motorola had driven to fourth place in television unit sales, only a fraction off the pace set by the industry leaders.

"Earned Security and Serving the Future"
16

The importance of his own brand name and all it stood for was a precious asset to Galvin. More than one critical decision related to the name "Motorola" was faced and overcome in the formative years of the company.

The first product branded as Motorola was the car radio. It was sold through the distributors and through dealers to the "after market" as an accessory, purchased after the car buyer took delivery of his automobile.

Most new automotive ideas were launched in those days as accessories rather than as a direct original sale offering by the car manufacturer. Headlights, trunks, spare tires, bumpers, all started as accessories before they became part of standard equipment on the car.

By the middle 1930s, the car manufacturers took notice of the fact that Motorola was popularizing and really selling auto radio. From 34,000 auto sets produced in 1930 and 145,000 in 1932, the industry jumped to 780,000 in 1934 and 1,190,000 in 1935. The car manufacturers decided to begin furnishing radios themselves as optional equipment.

In looking for a source of supply some of these manufacturers turned first to Motorola. Galvin politely refused each inquiry and proposal until a major car manufacturer made him an offer in 1935 that he had to consider.

He was promised a large and immediate increase in sales volume, assuring security for his

still small company in the years ahead. There
would be no credit or financing problems.

The disadvantages were that the manufacturer would not use the Motorola name. The demands of this market might prevent Galvin from
adequately handling the requirements of his distributors. He might become a private label producer again, more secure economically than he
had ever been but losing the brand identification
he had so arduously built up.

He spent many hours pondering the decision
he had to make. After the lean and uncertain
years, the struggle and the business failures, financial security would be welcome. There would
never be any question that if he accepted the
manufacturer's proposal he would always be able
to provide amply for his family. To achieve this
security he would have to sacrifice those things he
had worked so hard to achieve, not the least of
which was his distributor organization, made up
of many friends.

Once again he and Lillian and Bob made a
trip that would vitally affect their future. As they
had driven to Atlantic City in 1930, they drove
now to Detroit, and while Bob and Lillian waited
in the car, Galvin went into the conference with
the car manufacturing executives to give them his
decision. Until that moment, he was not sure what
that decision would be.

"One of the hardest decisions of my life," he
told a friend years later. "I guess I was wearier

than I realized and the secure road looked attractive.''

When he returned to the family in the car that day he told them quietly that he had turned down the car company's business and decided to ride with his own product and his own distributors.

''Wasn't any doubt in my mind you made the right choice then,'' one of his distributors told him years later at a sales meeting.

''That's a fine example of hindsight,'' Galvin smiled.

But by 1947 conditions had changed. The distributors whom Galvin did not want undermined in 1935 by 1947 were well established. By that time, the diversity of Motorola products made their franchise a valuable asset. And the car manufacturers had established themselves as the biggest single outlet for auto radios.

More and more automobiles were being sold with the radios installed. This fact was particularly true in the first postwar years when new cars were still scarce and the car dealer could convince his customers to accept them loaded with extras.

Galvin and Wavering, who was in charge of auto radio sales in 1947, realized that their distributors were preempted from a large part of the auto radio market. They reasoned that it would be advantageous for Motorola to earn a position as an original equipment supplier. The additional volume would help the company remain a low cost producer of all its products.

In the midst of their efforts to try and sell
"Detroit," an event of significance allowed Motorola a major break. The Detrola Company in Detroit, with a contract to make auto radios for
Ford Motor Company, was having serious work
stoppages and product sabotaging. The Detrola-
Ford problem became an open secret in the industry. Detrola was losing money and Ford was
not being supplied with the radios they required.

"There is a chance for us here," Galvin told
a few of his top automotive people, "if we move
fast and can work out a deal."

The management of Detrola and Galvin arranged a meeting. "We'll buy you out, lock stock
and barrel," Galvin told them, "subject only to
Ford's willingness to give us a chance as supplier
after the current model year."

When Ford agreed, Galvin moved quickly to
meet the demands of the contract. The plan to
make the switch as effortless as possible and prevent any possible sabotage was for Detrola to
post notices on its bulletin boards late Friday
afternoon stating that the plant would not reopen
Monday. Motorola moved crews into the Detrola
plant on Friday night and worked rapidly
through the weekend removing benches, tools, and
inventory. This material was all moved by truck
and reset in the company's Chicago plant so
that on Monday morning, with experienced operators waiting to go to work, Motorola picked up
the schedule without the loss of a single receiver.

This coup became the wedge which moved Motorola into an ever widening share of the auto radio business. In the years that followed, the company would produce 50 per cent of all the Ford and Chrysler car radio business and all of the American Motors requirements. General Motors, through its subsidiary, Delco Radio Division, made its own auto radios. And yet because of the quality of its product, Motorola was able to continue in the after market radio business as well, and has continued to serve its distributors also with auto radio merchandise through this entire period.

By 1950, Motorola's growth had been phenomenal. With the beginning of the Korean War on June 25, 1950, the company was able to move quickly into accelerated military production, and in a short period of time had almost 1,600 employees engaged in military work. At the same time, the demand of the consumer market spiraled wildly. People were once more fearful of the return of wartime restrictions, rationing, and the scarcity of goods. They bought in a frantic anticipation of shortages.

Motorola's sales jumped from $82 million in 1949 to a little over $177 million in 1950. By 1951, when it did not appear there would be any massive switch back to the rationing of the Second World War, the demand fell sharply and sales for the company dropped to $135 million.

With the end of the Korean War on July 27,

1953, a period of growth and expansion seemed apparent. Among other things, the company's work in civilian two-way radio for police, fire, and industrial use was attaining both leadership and important volume. Consumers were anxious for new products and new adaptations. A flurry of excitement over the prospects for color television swept the industry and the public.

By 1954, the company's sales passed $205 million and Motorola was well established in the black and white television receiver business, running at least fourth in unit production.

The industry had gone through a long and bitter battle from 1942 until December, 1953, over what basic technical standards would govern color television. From the start, Motorola had backed the compatible standards (able to receive broadcasts in black and white as well as color) adopted by RCA instead of the CBS incompatible design, though Motorola engineers had working models of the CBS system in operation before the war.

Having tasted the success of a bold move on black and white in 1947–48, Galvin remained alert to an opportunity to move up a notch or two in industry position when color TV came along. Conditions started to fit together that suggested to him another such coup could be pulled off.

RCA, whose system won out, tooled up for a "shadow mask" picture tube with a 15-inch round screen and in March, 1954 put their first color receivers on the market at $995 for the one console model. CBS, whose incompatible system was turned down by the Federal Communications Commission, had hedged its bet and also designed a compatible shadow mask tube with a 19-inch round screen. They were willing to produce this "large screen" tube if a substantial set manufacturer would commit itself to use the CBS "colortron" tube.

Motorola studied the CBS tube, then made the commitment. The company determined on a plan and strategy of being first to introduce and market large screen color under $1000—in fact, $895. Although both Galvin and his son Bob, then executive vice president, favored the decision and helped develop the program, there was a strong vocal dissent elsewhere in the Motorola management.

"Is the time right for color?" they asked.

Galvin responded with a question of his own, "When is the time?" and then provided the answer himself, "The time is now!"

He believed the biggest obstacle, the lack of a satisfactory tube, had been eliminated by CBS. The other deterrent, the scarcity of color shows, would be corrected in the fall, he felt, when color programming was scheduled to be stepped up.

But the time wasn't right. Insufficient color programs, service complications, a tube that was simply not good enough, and the high price of the

sets combined to suppress the market. Finally in
1956, with no major product change or other improvements looming soon on the horizon, a chastened Galvin withdrew from color TV to await
more favorable circumstances. He turned his attention to other promising areas of consumer
products. Spurred by his urging, the company
plunged boldly into the hi-fi phonograph business
in 1955.

*   *   *   *

In the first years following the Second World
War, Galvin was not only concentrating on putting
a competitive burr under the industry's saddle,
but felt that along with sound engineering and
research, one of the firmest ways to insure growth
was to substantially increase the stake of the employees in the company.

Even during the period from 1939 to 1947
when he was distributing liberal bonuses, Galvin was wary of how effective this practice was in
promoting employee security. He knew that all too
often the money was spent as soon as it was received. In 1940, he suggested to Joe that a program be drawn up to counteract this spending by
giving a limited number of their people an opportunity to vote for continued bonuses or a retirement plan. This plan, which they drafted and presented to their executives, was to Galvin's dismay
voted down.

But he continued urgently to stress the need
for a plan that would ''serve the future for all

Motorola employees.'' He did not believe that his employees deserved this security as an intrinsic right, but rather only as they earned it. He always spoke of such a plan as offering ''earned security'' with the emphasis on the ''earned.'' As an example of his attitude, from the start he was cool toward the concept of Federal Social Security. He believed that a creeping dependence on the government for security would ultimately sap initiative and contribute to the erosion of the private enterprise society and its vital freedoms. At the same time he believed that private organizations had a grave responsibility to both social and security ends.

George MacDonald, at that time Motorola's financial vice president, and Galvin investigated profit sharing plans then in existence. Galvin was not satisfied with most of them. They did not offer the measure of security he felt such a plan should contain. Finally, after consultation with advisors and legal assistants, a plan was formalized and drawn up.

Galvin decided to describe the Profit Sharing Plan to all employees and their families at a series of five evening meetings at a local hall. Galvin deemed the whole matter of great enough significance to want to handle the announcement personally.

At thirty minutes past the appointed hour of the first meeting, there were sixteen present of the two thousand who had been invited. Galvin was

thunderstruck and a little angry thinking that he
had been dealt a personal rebuff.

"What does this mean?" he asked Bob. "Are
they telling me I can go to hell?"

Bob, equally puzzled and concerned, suggested in the absence of any other explanation
that the evening's rain was responsible for the
poor attendance.

"Rain, my foot," Galvin said. "I want to
know first thing tomorrow morning if we've got a
revolution on our hands. Now I'm going to outline
the plan to the sixteen people who were good
enough to come."

In the morning Bob had Works Manager
Walter Scott assign his foremen to check with
their employees for the reasons they had not
attended the meeting. The foremen reported
back to Walter Scott and he carried the report to
Bob.

"The men simply did not see the need for any
meeting," he told Bob. "They were almost unani-
mous in saying that if P.V. felt the Profit Sharing
Plan was for their benefit, they didn't see any reason for a meeting."

It was a phenomenal demonstration of faith
in Galvin's judgment. He received the foremen's
report and justified it on the basis that considerable information on the proposed plan had been
distributed to the employees for weeks before the
meeting. But he could not conceal the fact that he
was gratified and moved. The balance of the meet-

VT-71, the industry's first television receiver under $200

Executives Ken Piper, Elmer Wavering, and
Ed Vanderwicken join Virginia Galvin to admire 25th Anniversary
memento presented by employees at company picnic

Very Reverend James T. Hussey, president of Loyola University, on occasion of honorary Doctor of Laws degree, June 10, 1951

With Cardinal Stritch and Father McGuire at Dinner to raise funds for Stritch Medical School, Chicago, December 12, 1957

Electronics Industry Association's
highest award, the Gold Medal,
presented by H. Leslie Hoffman,
president of the association,
at Chicago Convention, June 14, 1956

Paul and Virginia at Service Club Banquet,
Phoenix, Arizona, November 27, 1954

Reunion of Paul and Virginia
with Raymond (Burley) Galvin and sister, Helen

ings were cancelled and a descriptive pamphlet was distributed. On the day for conversion to the new plan, all but two employees signed it.

Galvin was warned that the company was still relatively small in a competitive industry and that forcing it to meet a regular financial obligation each year might endanger his position. Instead of tempering his approach, Galvin approved a company contribution to the Profit Sharing Fund of 20 per cent of earnings before taxes, after a minimum return to the company related to net worth. This was a startlingly liberal amount by the standards already existing in the field. As one of his competitors told Galvin with impatience, "You will get so damn generous with your heart that someday you'll give up running the company with your head."

The Employee Savings and Profit Sharing Fund became effective December 1, 1947, with 2,067 members. By the end of 1959, the year Galvin died, the fund was worth over $45 million, and a charter member who had contributed the maximum of $200 per year through the first twelve years had a vested account value of over $16,000. For his savings contribution of $2,400 in those twelve years, the fund had benefited the participant almost $14,000! It is estimated that by the plan's twenty-fifth birthday in 1972, typical charter members will have an account value of over $50,000.

The Motorola Profit Sharing Plan, which became a model for many similar plans adopted by

other firms, was the new bedrock on which Galvin
continued to build a stronger and more com-
prehensive human relations program in the company. He had always been concerned with the welfare of his people but by 1947 with employment
reaching almost 5,000, he began to realize that the
"Motorola" family had grown to a size that a for-
malization of emphasis on the "human" approach was necessary.

Galvin would have much preferred the old
free exchange of personal contact, but for some
time he had not been able to remember the first
names of each and every one of his 5,000 employees. He could no longer be personally cogni-
zant of the welfare of each one of them. In 1949
he set up a human relations department at the corporate level headed by Kenneth Piper, a seasoned
industrial relations executive. Now he could rest
assured that wage rates, fringe benefits, recrea-
tion programs, publications, and the many other
services to people would be consistently under re-
view. Yet, he constantly stressed the need to keep
these services "personal," to prevent them from
becoming mere rules in a service booklet.

All this time, Galvin did not neglect his obligation to the community outside the boundaries of
the company. He served as a member of the board
of directors of the Evanston Hospital Association, Marillac House, and was a member of the
President's Council at Loyola University. By
order of Pope Pius XII he was designated a

Knight of Malta and a Knight of Saint Gregory, two of the highest awards that can be presented to a Catholic layman.

On one occasion, the Catholic Cardinal in Chicago was faced with a partial failure of an important fund-raising dinner for the medical school at Loyola University. Two weeks before the dinner, Galvin called a number of his friends and requested of each of them the task of assembling a quota of people. A week before the dinner, it was completely sold out. To further encourage the Cardinal, he also underwrote anonymously the complete cost of the affair—some $16,000. That evening the Cardinal expressed his appreciation to "our unnamed benefactor."

He particularly liked to work with the Sisters. He used to say of one of them, "If she had only been a man I would have wanted her as an officer of my company."

He was also a great one to bet on individuals. There was no record kept of the many young men and women he helped through a year or two of college. He realized from his own experience what a boost such support could be.

Outside of his family, Motorola was the essence of his life. Unlike many other prominent men in Chicago whose service toward the community he greatly admired, he did not lean toward a prominent position in civic affairs. He never assumed a major city-wide fund drive. He felt that he could best do his part by concentrating his

efforts on creating jobs and creating markets and
that public affairs would be best served thereby.

Yet, in spite of this, he received in 1951 an
honorary Doctor of Laws degree from Loyola
University. In 1956, the Electronics Industry Association voted him its Medal of Honor, the association's highest award for outstanding contributions to the industry. In awarding him the medal,
the EIA president said, "Few men have the vitality and capacity that have enabled Paul Galvin
to devote so much time to activities of broad
industry interest while at the same time building
up a business from scratch to a multi-million
dollar corporation. Yet he never seems hurried or
harried."

"The Future
Is My Son"
17

Many men dream boundless visions for their sons. They visualize these children as extensions of their own lives, reaching beyond them to a place they had not reached. A father lives in his son in a way a son can never live in his father, and because of this ancient incompatibility, there is often disappointment and despair. Sometimes there is triumph and fulfillment.

Galvin and Lillian had only one child, a son, born on October 9, 1922 in Marshfield, Wisconsin, not too long before the battery company failed. When less than a year old, the boy, Robert, made the dismal journey from Marshfield to Chicago with his parents. When he was eight he went along on the fateful trip to Atlantic City and was a silent passenger in the rear seat of the car as Galvin, and sometimes Lillian, pressed the merits of the still unproven car radio to the less than enthusiastic distributors.

Galvin was fearful of the false and graceless sin of pride and yet he loved Bob greatly and all of his life was proud of him.

It was true that in the first years of the company, desperately trying to keep the business alive, there was little time for Galvin to spend with his son. There were many evenings when Bob and his mother ate dinner alone.

On Sunday afternoons, when Galvin was not on the road, he would take Bob for a walk around the lagoon in Garfield Park. Then for a while they visited a fire station together. They would get on

the Washington Boulevard bus and ride all the
way to the fire station on Canal and Washington,
next to the Northwestern Depot. They visited this
station every Sunday for months and came to
know the firemen who would let Bob climb on the
engines and sit behind the majestic wheels. As a
climax one of the firemen would slide down the
pole with the boy. This experience was their undo-
ing for on one such descent Bob hit his head as
they slid past one of the intermediate floors. The
battalion chief put an end to further adventures.

The Sunday afternoons they spent together
gained a special significance for both of them, in
some ways as much pleasure for the father as they
were for the son. Galvin had bought Bob a complete fireman's outfit and days to be particularly
remembered came when, with Bob in his uniform,
they discovered a fire in progress. They would
maneuver as close as they could to the firefighting
equipment and men and shout their own orders
masked by the noise. Almost thirty-five years
later, Bob could recall these excursions and remember the immense delight they provided him.

As the boy grew older, Galvin began to take
him along on some of the business trips he made.
One of their trips was by boat, a paddle wheeler
that traveled on the lake.

These trips together were part of the way in
which Galvin sought to compensate for the scarcity of time they could spend together. In some
more subtle ways, perhaps, he was acquainting

the boy with his own feeling about the value of purposeful motion. He had a strong sense of wanting the boy drawn into the thread and fabric of the business that was so much a part of his own life, so much his own dreams as a boy, and also indefinably tied into movement across the land. The traveling on train, bus and plane was a way of allowing a nine-year-old to share in the experience. Even in the case of the old paddle wheeler, he told his son, ''I want you to go on this boat and sleep overnight, because this kind of a boat won't exist very much longer. I just want you to have this experience.''

Sometimes, during a business conference, the son sat off in a corner, quietly waiting for his father, listening to words and a terminology that were beyond his understanding then, but undoubtedly absorbing something of the atmosphere, the urgency and ardor of a salesman selling his product. It was as if Galvin calculated, with a stern and compelling zest, the value of such an exposure for his son.

In the same way, they shared a number of school experiences together. When Bob, in one of the early elementary grades, was having difficulty with arithmetic, Galvin sat down with him and patiently devised a game of competition around the problems. They were pitted against one another, so that solution for his son became a kind of victory.

Another experience between father and son

took place when the boy was in the fourth or fifth grade and concerned a seemingly impossible assignment to the boy. Bob had to prepare a report on the steel industry. The primary source for this information was an encyclopedia, which in those depression days they did not own, and which would have been too difficult for a fourth or fifth grader to understand. Galvin began calling acquaintances on the phone until he had located one who owned an encyclopedia and prevailed upon him to read portions of the text over the telephone while Galvin copied it down. Then he sought to transcribe this text into language that the boy could understand and use in preparing his own report.

"Even small problems seem big when they are not solved," Galvin would say in later years. "Making an effort to solve them keeps them small."

The family lived for a while on Marshfield Avenue west of the Harrison Street Plant and then moved to the north side of Chicago and lived in an apartment in Rogers Park. It was not until 1934 that Galvin bought the home on Normandy Place in Evanston which presaged a rise in the fortunes of the family. Lillian had discovered the house by driving up and down the streets she and Galvin had selected. When she saw a house she liked, she went up boldly and rang the bell to inquire if the house was for sale. One lady, surprised at the timeliness of her inquiry, said,

"Yes, but we haven't even put it on the market yet." Three weeks later the transaction was completed.

Galvin was not a man who cared to do handy-work about the house or in the garden, but preferred to spend the time quietly in the company of those he cared for. Their circle of friends, outside of the family, was small but close. The holidays were particularly festive affairs, and with increasing frequency, their home was the site of intimate gay parties.

Perhaps remembering their austere early years, Lillian planned these parties with enthusiasm. Galvin would say of her efforts with admiration, "She could really pick 'em up and lay 'em down." Above all else, both of them liked parties at which things were happening—games, poker, and especially dancing.

Lillian was a slim, lovely and petite woman with abundant sparkle. Her relationship with Galvin was remarkably close with few disruptive arguments or disagreements. She was not reluctant to offer him business advice and it was usually sound. If Galvin was a bulwark for her, it was just as true that she was a source of inspiration to him. Most of all she was a zestful and gay companion. They went to the theatre together and once or twice a month dined and danced at one of the finer Chicago hotels. These were evenings they both enjoyed.

"When a man and woman have shared the

hardship that Lillian and I have shared,'' Galvin
said once to a close friend, ''there are not words
that can easily describe how much they come to
mean to one another.''

He sent her a thoughtful tribute on each of
her birthdays. She spoke of one particular time
when for no apparent reason he sent her a bright
bouquet of roses and a card which simply read,
''With all my eternal gratitude and love.''

In the early thirties, Galvin interested Bob
in golf, a game at which Galvin was not accomplished but which he played with vigor and determination. He had taken lessons from a local golf
pro and arranged for Bob to have lessons as well.
They both looked forward eagerly to the weekend
when they could play together. Although young-
sters under twelve were not permitted to play that
particular course, and Bob was eleven, they overcame this obstacle by having Bob carry his father's clubs through the first green, play the
following sixteen holes, then carry the clubs again
to finish the eighteenth. Since they played very
early in the morning, when the course was almost
empty, they rationalized that this deception was
not too serious an infraction of the rules.

Although it slowed down the pace of his own
game, Galvin did not mind taking the boy along.
By playing as ably as he could and giving no
quarter, he spurred the boy on to greater effort.
By 1938 and 1939, the shoe was on the other foot.
Bob, by this time, had developed a proficiency to

beat his father as regularly as his father had once beaten him. While Galvin was pleased that Bob had become a good golfer, his own natural competitiveness made it uncomfortable for him to accept second place, and he fought as aggressively as he could.

He never really became, for all of his effort and will, a good golfer and this was a source of great concern to him. "Why can't I beat that game?" he would say heatedly in later years. "I have done anything else I set my mind to do but I just can't seem to improve my game to a point where it would satisfy me."

When Bob graduated from his parochial elementary school, Galvin recommended and Bob agreed that he should attend the local public high school to permit him a broader acquaintance with students of varied interests and faiths.

Through this period, Galvin also sought to stimulate Bob into activities that he thought would be beneficial for the boy, with deceptively casual suggestions. "Well, I think that would be worthwhile," or, "Maybe you ought to try that. You think about it and do what you want."

Galvin could not conceal his zealous enthusiasm for public speaking. "Learning how to handle yourself before people," he told Bob, "learning how to speak—this will be greatly helpful to you."

Following his pattern of being as sparing with his praise as he was in his business, Galvin did not shower compliments on Bob for work well done. He quietly assumed they both knew what needed to be done, what was best, and then he hoped Bob's work in school would naturally reflect this assumption. He remained as unobtrusively in the background as he could, letting the boy make his own way but hovering close if there was any need to offer counsel or help.

"His son grew the way his business grew," an associate of Galvin's said. "He gave the boy his head and yet he was never far away."

And a close friend of the family said, "Galvin tried not to show how much that boy meant to him. But when he talked to us about something Bob had done well, a light of really fierce pride and love came into his eyes."

Galvin wished dearly that his son would want to enter the business. But he had also suffered disappointment before. He was determined not to succumb to the illusion of the usual parental expectation only to have this dream shattered when Bob decreed an alternate direction of his own. Despite his uncertainty about the outcome, and for all of his efforts to exercise restraint, Galvin worked to prepare Bob for the responsibility of moving into the company.

He would answer his son's questions about the business with great patience and considerable detail. At the dinner table in the evening, he would discuss the business events of the day with him. When he was preparing a speech for delivery before some industry group, he would ask Bob to take a look at the draft. "I'm going to give this speech," he would say. "I'd be grateful if you look it over and let me have your suggestions." And, often, he'd accept them.

The culmination of the years of hoping and planning came at the January 11, 1940, Motorola distributor convention at the Edgewater Beach Hotel in Chicago when Galvin introduced Bob to the assembled distributors and a few key Motorola employees for the first time. The company was celebrating its twelfth birthday and the tenth anniversary of auto radio. The morning and afternoon had been spent introducing the new product lines and the windup was an elaborate banquet in the evening.

Galvin had very casually mentioned to Bob a week before that sometime during the course of the evening he would introduce him to the distributors and that Bob might acknowledge the introduction by "saying just a few words." What response Bob would make he left up to him.

Bob was seventeen at the time, a senior in high school, an excellent student, a good athlete and already a confident extemporaneous speaker, but this evening marked his first formal exposure to the men who sold the Motorola line of products.

The night of the banquet, Bob sat at the speaker's table between his father and Elmer Wavering. Galvin's nervousness was apparent to his old friends, obviously not nervousness for himself because such banquets were an old and familiar business. But he was aware of the significance of the introduction of his son and the response the boy would make and how it would be received.

When the moment came for him to speak, Galvin rose, and after looking once to where his wife, Lillian, stood hidden behind a backdrop in the wings of the room, he began with an evident tremor in his voice. He spoke of the forming of the company, of the hard road they had struggled, of where they hoped to go. He spoke of his gratefulness to Joe and to the men who worked beside him. Then with an intensely dramatic gesture, he pointed to his son. "Some of you have asked me about the future," he said. "I want to introduce you to the future. I want you to meet my son."

Galvin sat down drained for the moment of emotion, and Bob rose. There is no written record of the words he spoke then, but the impression that remains in the memory of all who heard him is of a quiet and simple, yet marvelously moving tribute to his father, and of the guidance and love he was grateful to have received from him. When Bob had finished, the response was a long and thunderous ovation. Every man rose to his feet, contributing something to the din.

It was perhaps true as one man present recalled that the assembled men were waiting to be moved, that any tribute to Galvin, who was beloved by all of them, would have met with enthusiastic response. But it was also true that they sensed the high drama of the moment and each vicariously shared it with the father and the son.

For Galvin it was one of the great moments of his life, a moment to be compared with his jubilant return to America from France at the end of the First World War, with his marriage to Lillian, and with the birth of their son, a moment when the course of life around him seemed beneficent and profound.

"Learn As Much As You Can ... Use That Knowledge Soundly"
18

Bob first joined the company on June 18, 1940, at the age of seventeen, in the stockroom of the plant on Augusta Boulevard. On his first day, he sat in the personnel office awaiting his turn among other new employees. One of the personnel people recognized him and asked him to come right in, but Bob waited his turn.

His first few weeks in the stockroom, under the tutelage of the wise and capable Gus Peters, seemed to provide him so much information that on Friday of the third week he sought an opportunity to tell Peters that he was now thoroughly familiar with the operation. He supposed it was time to move to another assignment. Whether by design or by accident, he could never quite get Peters alone. The weekend passed and by Monday he thought better of the situation. As the weeks became first a month and then two months, the stockroom operation grew more complex and Bob realized with considerable chagrin how hasty his original presumption had been. Years later, he would tell this story to disgruntled young men who felt they had exhausted the potential of their departments, not to discourage them from wishing to move up but to remind them to reassure themselves that they had realized the maximum benefit from their responsibilities. For Bob the experience had been a sobering one, and he remained working in the stockroom for the balance of the summer.

In the fall, he entered the University of Notre Dame as a freshman to study commerce.

The following summer of 1941, with the tension of the expanding war reflected in frantic efforts of industry to prepare, Bob returned to work in the Motorola inspection department.

By the summer of 1942, Bob had decided not to return to Notre Dame for the beginning of his junior year. This decision was made for a number of reasons and arrived at reluctantly since he had been an excellent student scholastically, in the upper ten per cent of his class. But he was anxious to prepare himself more effectively for military service and that fall enrolled in MIT to study engineering. After one week, he realized the futility of remaining in school in a passive role. He returned home to enter the struggle in a more personal capacity and enlisted in the Army Signal Corps Training Program.

Through the autumn of 1942, he lived at home while attending special Signal Corps classes in the Chicago loop. On the night of Thursday, October 22, 1942, he returned home from school to discover the bodies of his mother, Lillian, and a young maid, Edna Sibilski, murdered by a prowler or prowlers they had apparently surprised in the act of robbing the house. It was a terrible and shattering experience for the young man.

Galvin, traveling en route from Washington to Chicago, could not be reached at once, but early

Friday morning at Fort Wayne, Indiana, Frank
Brach and his wife boarded the Chicago-bound
train to carry the dreadful news to him in his
compartment. They rode with him to the 63d St.
station where Bob and several of his friends
awaited him.

Of all the tragedies Galvin had suffered in his
life, this senseless and brutal murder of his beloved wife was the hardest for him to understand
and sustain. In addition, he grieved for his son,
and sorrowed for the family of the young maid, a
girl in her early twenties, who had been engaged
to be married.

After the funeral, he felt that he could not
continue to live in the house on Normandy Place
and moved with Bob into an apartment at the
Edgewater Beach Hotel. By an arduous effort, he
continued to meet his responsibilities at Motorola
and his duties as president of the RMA but his
friends and associates in this period speak of the
dark depression which he sustained for almost a
year. He did what actually had to be done in the
course of his business, but beyond that refrained
from all social contact except with the immediate
members of the family. Bob was a source of concern to him, because the tragedy had impaired the
young man's health, and in the months following
the murder, he developed a severe ulcer which
forced him to accept a medical discharge from the
Signal Corps.

It was a dark and forbidding period for both father and son, a time when they tried to protect and console one another, to shield each other from the silences that prompted recall of the past.

It was also a dark and critical time of national struggle with the very survival of the country at stake. The fighting in the Pacific and in the Far East was the bloodiest of the war as the United States fought to regain the territories she had lost in the first months following the attack upon Pearl Harbor. The early part of 1943 continued the pattern of capturing Japanese-held islands, one by one, only after savage and prolonged fighting. The landings and final victory over the heavily fortified Japanese positions on Tarawa cost one division alone, the U.S. 2d Marine Division, almost 1,000 dead and several thousand more wounded.

Perhaps this awareness of the countless personal tragedies being endured by so many other families more than anything else helped Galvin measure and accept his own loss. A day came when he and Bob packed their belongings and returned to their house on Normandy Place. "It was Lillian's home, our home," Galvin told a friend quietly. "We shared many wonderful memories there that counted for more than what happened in the end."

Lillian's sister, Rose Sturm, herself a widow unselfishly gave up her apartment and moved in

with them for the next year to help re-establish a
home.

*   *   *   *

For the balance of 1943 and into 1944 Galvin
drove himself with a consuming energy and effort
to meet his multiple responsibilities as the head of
Motorola and as the president of the RMA.

Bob rotated jobs in the plants acquiring as
much experience as he could, doing everything
from nailing crates on the packing line to acting as
a trouble-shooter eliminating production bottlenecks. For some months during this period, he
also occupied a place in a corner of Dan Noble's
laboratory where he received a concentrated and
intensive course in radio and electronics.

"I am concerned that you learn as much as
you can," Galvin told Bob, "and that you use that
knowledge soundly when you are called upon to
make decisions." And to an associate who suggested that he appoint Bob a vice president before his twenty-first birthday, Galvin answered,
"I am not concerned about his age as much as I
am concerned that he be capable of assuming the
responsibilities."

Galvin knew that the company faced a hard
road through the balance of the war and into the
post-war market. He understood that the growth
of the company between 1941 and 1943, an increase in sales from $17 million to $78 million, did
not truly reflect the potential of the company in

the post-war market. By 1943, Motorola production was entirely for the military. In any change-over, he figured, the sales could slip back momentarily to the pre-war figure. And while there had been a $61 million rise in sales in the two year period, the corresponding increase in net earnings had only been an additional $353,500.

"This tight and controlled market," he told a group of his executives, "tells us nothing about the pattern we will have to meet later on."

Joe Galvin's death on March 7, 1944, at the age of 45 dealt another severe blow to the family. It was tragic for Joe's wife and his three children because he was still a comparatively young husband and father. But following as it did less than two years after the death of his wife, Galvin felt the loss with terrible force.

Perhaps for the first time in his life, he became apprehensive of the future. The death of his wife and his brother brought him face to face with his own mortality. He was fearful that the company Joe and he had worked so hard to build would not survive, because he would not survive.

He had the consolation of his strong faith but he had also learned through experience the tenuous grasp any man held on life. He began to be more fervently aware of time, felt it uneasily within him, a goad to all the things that were still undone. He was concerned not only with the business but with the family. "If I die," Galvin told

Bob, "watch out for our old relatives." And he
began to think more insistently in terms of Bob
assuming more of the responsibility.

There were those within the company who
felt that Bob was also needed to balance the swing
of some of his father's impatient decisions. There
were complaints during this time that Galvin
would not tolerate opposition to anything he had
made up his mind to do. The zestful atmosphere
of open opinion and informal discussion which he
had championed, and which up to that time had
prevailed, was now restricted. Suddenly, few of
the executives dared to disagree with him for fear
of arousing a flare of unreasonable anger.

"If I want your opinion," he irately told a
manager who had interrupted him during a meeting, "I'll ask for it." And to another who opposed
him he said angrily, "We didn't bring you in here
to find out how inflexible you are!" Sometimes his
irritation provoked him into a general condemna-
tion, something he had always scorned in the past
as not constructive. "Why don't you guys do
some thinking for yourselves?" he flared impatiently at a session of his top people.

Of all the people in the company and the close
friends outside his business, it was only Bob who
had a constant closeness of contact and a license
of disagreement with his father far outweighing
his own position in the company at that time.

In some of the disputes between them, the
positions of the generations were frequently

strangely reversed, with the father restless and impatient to get something done, and the son cautioning objectivity and restraint. Yet more often than not the course of events proved Galvin right.

This give and take between father and son, this capacity to achieve a certain harmony and clarity through disagreement, profited both of them, and especially Bob. He had always had a massive respect and affection for his father. He also came to understand more clearly that part of his father's strength and the reason for his achievement lay in a kind of intuitive brilliance as to the right move to make at a certain time, something that could not be acquired by a man if he went through all the graduate business courses in the world.

Much of Galvin's distress through this period came quite simply because he was lonely. He had enjoyed few interests outside of his business and his family. The loss of Lillian had left an unhappy void in his life.

In the fall of 1944, Galvin met a poised and lovely young lady. Her name was Virginia Critchfield and she worked as a secretary in his physician's office. On visits to the doctor's office during the late months of 1944 and the early months of 1945, Galvin was impressed with Virginia's warmth and sense of humor.

In the spring of 1945, he suggested he be allowed to escort her to a play that same evening. He had forgotten the propriety of advance notice a lady requires and she returned her regrets. A week later he asked her again and provided two weeks of notice. She accepted and they began to meet for dinner and an occasional play. Later that summer, he began taking Virginia to some of the Motorola functions such as the Foremen's Banquet and the Glee Club Concert.

On other evenings that summer, Galvin would visit Virginia at the home of her artist sister, Carol Critchfield. They would sit on the front porch in the evening sipping tea and these were moments of great serenity for Galvin after the turmoil of his day. He enjoyed these visits immensely, and his affection for Virginia grew. At the end of one such evening he told her with a certain shyness and yet ardently, "I delight in your company." On November 21, 1945, Galvin and Virginia were married in a quiet ceremony at home. A new and lasting happiness had entered his life.

Galvin was a cheerful and buoyant husband and never permitted Virginia to become bored or melancholy. He continued to court her after their marriage. He sent her flowers often and he would turn from his work during the day to phone her a number of times. With his active imagination, he would assume the voices of various characters in a charade of stories that enchanted her. In the evenings, they went dancing together, attended the theatre or the opera, and sometimes spent the evening with friends.

The hours he enjoyed the most were those he spent with Virginia at home. He would remain in his pajamas, robe, and slippers until early Saturday afternoon, talking to his executives by phone on proposals that had occurred to him since the day before. Between calls he would relax at the electric organ which he had laboriously taught himself to play. Virginia would sit with him while he proudly played a medley of songs they both enjoyed.

It was evident to many who knew him well and worked with him in this period of the late 1940s and early 1950s that he was a man at the peak of his powers. Certainly the market from the end of the war through the Korean war, despite momentary setbacks, was a rampantly good one. He was, in addition, immensely benefited by a group of engineers and managers who could think as individuals and function brilliantly as a team.

Yet for all of this able assistance, Galvin was undeniably the one person most singularly responsible for the incredible growth of the company during those years: from 1,500 employees and $31 million sales in 1942 to 10,000 employees and $168 million sales in 1952.

In November of 1948, satisfied that the intense period of orientation and diverse responsibility had qualified him, Galvin made Bob executive vice president and placed him in an office adjoining his own so they might work even more closely together. But up to the hour of the appointment, he remained the relentless and uncompromising taskmaster. Hearing of a decision that displeased him, a decision that Bob bore responsibility for, he called his son into his office and peremptorily told him, "You know that appointment I was getting ready to announce? Well the whole thing is off."

His feeling did not last for long. The appointment was an extremely important one for both father and son. It gave Bob the opportunity to introduce and implement more directly his own thinking into the company.

Yet there is always tension when the new seeks to break into a movement and purpose of its own. Galvin and Bob were no exception to this tension but they were fortunate in that the communion of their years together, particularly the tragedy they had shared, gave them a reserve of patience and trust. To this attribute, Bob added a willingness to accept what his father had built, and he did not feel compelled to replace his father's accomplishments with something that would be his alone.

Galvin did not always find it easy to relinquish control or to leave a matter he thought important in the hands of someone else, even Bob. Hearing of a meeting in Bob's office he would sometimes walk into the middle of it and brusquely ask, "What's going on?" If the decisions of the meeting did not appear satisfactory to him, he would object, "That isn't the way it

should be at all!'' With the others silent and
occasionally cowed, Bob would begin quietly
to explain, ''Dad, before you came in we thought
it out this way,'' and then lead Galvin through the
sequence of reasons why the decision had been
made. More often convinced than not, Galvin would
willingly acknowledge their position.

There were often lessons for Bob to learn.
One morning, Galvin caught his son in the hall
and told him a competitor had just come out with
a TV set priced $20 under a comparable Motorola
leader model. In the highly competitive early television market, most possible reductions in the
price of receivers had already been realized. Galvin, in spite of this already tight margin, asked
Bob what he was going to do about the $20 differ-
ence while still satisfying the company tradition
of quality and profit. Bob's firm response was
that nothing could be done about it, that the price
of the set was already at rock-bottom.

''You go back there and find a way to knock
$20 off our leader set,'' Galvin said, ''or I'll step
in and show you how.''

Ten days later, after a series of meetings
with engineers and production people, Bob could
report sheepishly to his father that the reduction
had been accomplished.

Through a gradually evolving process, they
came to complement one another in a remarkable
way. Yet, there remained a basic difference between generations, a variance in the experience

that produced each of these men. Galvin ever mindful of his early struggles continued willing to drive for growth, depending upon emotion and intuition to direct his approach, but preferring to do it along tried and proven lines. Bob also felt that the company had to be progressive, but that it would be necessary to diversify into varied and new interests.

"If We Do This Thing...
Let's Do It Right"
19

Perhaps no development in the history of the company more clearly reflected the coordinating of Paul and Bob Galvin's philosophies than the decision to "go for broke" in the semiconductor business in Phoenix.

In 1948, Bell Laboratories announced the revolutionary "transistor," a tiny bit of germanium with hair-thin wire leads, enclosed in a metal cap about the size of a pencil eraser, which performed the same function as a vacuum tube.

Motorola initially entered the transistor field through the military laboratory in Phoenix in a relatively small way aimed at developing a few devices for use in the company's own products. In particular these were for the military, communications, home and auto radio products, which, it was then thought, would be vastly improved by the use of the more compact and reliable transistor. Meanwhile, a great competitive scramble on the part of many other firms to enter the transistor market was developing.

By the middle 1950s, the transistor operation, by then a separate activity in a plant of its own, had come to the crossroads. The venture would have to be vastly extended and financed or abandoned. But the decision to expand the project was a major one for Motorola and to Galvin it was fraught with danger. He did not feel completely comfortable in this particular electronics area, despite the confidence he felt in the abilities of

Dan Noble, his engineers, and the judgment of Bob.

Galvin's major objection, sternly reinforced by some of his executives, was that the company had been strictly an equipment manufacturing operation. They might be at a loss to calculate accurately the needs and requirements of the transistor and diode market. He felt correctly that there would be a tremendous drain on the other divisions' earnings for a good many years before any profit could be realized.

But Bob's feeling, militating for a dynamic expansion and staunchly supported by Noble, was that unless they were large enough they could not hope to afford enough research. If they continued to limit their production only to supply the other divisions of their company, they would lose the sharp stimulus of selling in a competitive market.

The key questions were, "Would requirements for semiconductors in Motorola products alone provide sufficient volume? Would it be enough to enable a semiconductor operation to support the research and engineering that could achieve the yields and costs necessary to a viable business?" The answer was that the volume for the company's demand alone would not be adequate to afford an engineering program to lead in the semiconductor art. Bob and Noble urged that the company had to serve successfully the much greater outside market to survive and attain leadership knowledge in this new technology.

Then the question was asked, "Can we succeed as a component supplier while continuing to grow as an equipment manufacturer?" It was true there would be areas of conflict. Motorola would sometimes find itself a competitor of a company while also attempting to be a supplier to it through the semiconductor products division. Hopefully, the component user looked for the fresh and better solution to his problems and would therefore buy from the best source regardless of this apparent conflict of interest. Motorola would have to maintain complete respect for the confidential relationship that must exist with each customer.

The final decision ruled in favor of the expansion and development of the semiconductor division, a major revising of the future direction of an important part of the company. It was to Galvin's credit that, although not at first completely convinced in his own mind of the soundness of this move, he became one of its strong supporters. "If we're going to do this thing," Galvin said, "let's do it right."

And doing it right required the building of a massive plant facility in Arizona with rapid and dynamic growth. Within a few years, the company had become the largest employer in the state and the leading supplier of certain power transistors, silicon zener diodes, and mesa transistors; along with the silicon automobile rectifiers, which made the Motorola automotive alternator, an AC power generator for automobiles, practical as a mass production item.

A brilliant staff of engineers, research specialists and business people paved the way for moves into the fields of solid state industrial controls and integrated circuitry. The latter product carried the development of the transistor into a wafer the size of a pin head which contains a complete electronic circuit.

By the middle 1950s, the company had become too big for a single man to continue making all of the major decisions. Galvin knew that this condition now existed and discussed the problem with Bob. The organizational pattern that evolved in their thinking was to reshape the entire company along product division lines.

Each division would be self-contained with its own engineering, purchasing, manufacturing and marketing departments. Such a structure was already effective in parts of the company, and they decided it was to become the company-wide policy and pattern. Each division was established as its own profit center. There was automotive under Elmer Wavering, and consumer products under Ed Taylor, to be joined in 1956 by a field-trained marketing manager, Ted Herkes. The communications, semiconductor, and military divisions were under Dan Noble's wing. Galvin mounted a conscious program of loosening the reins.

In November, 1956, reflecting Bob's successful transition from the responsibility of executive

To their associates they seemed
more like brothers than father and son

Bob presents twenty-five-year service pin
to his dad in 1953

The transfer of experience was a daily process

Robert W. Galvin elected president in 1956

vice president he had assumed in 1948, Galvin
and his board of directors named Bob Galvin
president of Motorola and named each of the division managers executive vice presidents. The
strong central system of the corporation sur-
rounding Bob included such seasoned executives
as Ed Vanderwicken, financial officer, and Walter
Scott, production officer. Galvin moved himself
up to chairman of the board and chief executive
officer. He understood that the company's growth
raised problems that could no longer be answered
by intuition and personal contact alone. The dy-
namics of the large corporation were different
from those upon which the small company relied.

But he was not at all ready for pasture. "Can
you ever imagine a day when you will retire?"
Matt Hickey asked him once.

"Never!" Galvin said.

Yet perhaps this relinquishing of more authority to his son and associates, proud fulfillment
of a dream though it was, touched Galvin with a
kind of sadness as well. It marked the passing of
an era he had known, a time when he could clearly
understand all the parts that composed the whole,
when a decision could be made because he "had a
hunch," when the basic design of a new line of
auto radio could be decided overnight by Wavering and himself sketching and smudging on a
restaurant tablecloth. Those personally involved
and jubilant days were gone.

Galvin had lived to see the company change.

He had come to understand the isolation which is forced upon the executive head of a large corporation, the environment as relentless as a prison within which he must function. Whether he willed it or not, he was becoming a prisoner of the size and of the complexity of his responsibility. Problems brought to him now were mostly reduced to a point where a "yes" or "no," or something approximating that, was all that was required. Yet, these decisions carried an awesome responsibility.

But now there was no time to examine all issues completely for himself. For all of his efforts he had become a depersonalized figure of the "boss" to thousands of his employees whom he could never really get to know anymore than they could ever really know him. If they were now partners in a common venture, there was nevertheless a wall between them, a wall that could not be breached, a wall behind which he must sit alone.

"Do Not Fear Mistakes ...
Reach Out"
20

Galvin had never been a particularly robust man physically. His compact body and vigorous voice had given the impression of a sturdiness but for most of his life and especially during the years of the middle 1950s, he was besieged by a series of minor ailments and some aggravated ones. He had stomach difficulty and had an emergency gall bladder operation. He had recurring back trouble and for varying periods of time he wore a brace. He was bothered by arthritis in his hands, and his feet would sometimes tingle and burn.

He would go from doctor to doctor hoping for relief from these varied disorders. At fairly frequent intervals he would have a medical checkup. He always returned from these examinations more fully informed of what was troubling him, but was not always helped. That he could see the wry humor of his situation was evidenced in something he said to his secretary, Jean Nohren, "A man is fine when he is up at Mayo's—what about after he comes back?"

In May of 1958, Galvin and Virginia, in company with their good friends, the Vincent Sills, visited the Greenbriar Hotel in White Sulphur Springs, West Virginia. Virginia had been troubled by black and blue marks on her arms and with his knowledge of medical symptoms, Galvin told her cautiously this might be a sign of leukemia. They both went through the clinic at Greenbriar. Virginia was given a clear bill of health but Galvin was found to be slightly anemic and in need of iron. There were inconclusive symptoms that it might be he who had leukemia. He felt the doctors must be mistaken.

In June of 1958, Galvin developed a hard respiratory infection and had difficulty breathing. He entered the hospital in Evanston and a series of blood tests taken by the hematologists confirmed the suspicions of the Greenbriar specialists. He was told the diagnosis of leukemia at the beginning but there were still areas of doubt and he was very hopeful that he could lick it. "I've got this blood thing," he said to a good friend, "and I've got to fight it."

He began a series of treatments that produced some improvement for brief periods and this heartened him. Doctors reported to him various new methods for improving the condition of his blood and he allowed these treatments upon him. There were temporary successes. The failures greatly outnumbered the successes but this concern did not seem to dampen his spirit. He could still joke about the situation. "They can't say that Paul Galvin isn't doing his bit for medical science," he said.

But by Christmas of 1958, Galvin was quite ill and had lost a good deal of weight. He went back into the hospital and remained until the beginning of March. He came out anxious to go to Phoenix, feeling that, "The change would do me good."

Virginia was apprehensive about taking him

away from his regular doctors, but deferring to his wishes, she finally agreed. In Phoenix, he played cards and rested and practiced on the putting green, but once a week he had to go to the hospital for a transfusion.

Early in April of 1959, they returned to Chicago. He entered the hospital again and was rested to an extent that he could emerge on May fourth to conduct his last stockholder's meeting. There he was presented with a silver bowl by Bob on behalf of the board of directors to honor him for his thirty years of service. With an obvious quaver in his voice Galvin told the assembled audience that he knew the company's next thirty years would be even more exciting than the three decades that he had passed.

After that, Galvin seemed to improve for a little while, but then entered a distressing period when he suffered from spells of severe weakness. He was bothered by sleeplessness, and at night restlessly roamed the house on Normandy Place. When he did manage to sleep, he was beset by a curious jerking in his legs that woke him again.

Perhaps in this time, too, his thinking underwent a change. The long months of struggle had roused the old fighter in him and he was fervent for victory, so determined in fact that he refused to acknowledge how slim were the reasons for any continued hope.

"A part of me wants to obey God's will," he said quietly to a friend. "But another part of me refuses to give up hope that I will become better if I fight hard enough.''

There were indeed times when he seemed to achieve all of his old force. The last distributor meeting he was to attend, on July 1, 1959 at the Drake Hotel, reunited him with many of the men he was so fond of, the friends he had known for so long.

Galvin's activity that day, and the confident forceful talk he delivered to them gave no hint to anyone of the severity of his condition. It was not until late in the afternoon when he confided to Virginia who had remained by his side, ''I'm tired now. I think we'd better go home.''

That summer, Bob Galvin with his family moved out to their new farm near Barrington, Illinois. They gave a housewarming party and invited a number of company executives to attend. Galvin insisted on being present as well. It rained and after a while the sky cleared into a serene and lovely summer night with a great moon low over the trees. Galvin sat in a chair beside the swimming pool. He was in a nostalgic mood and talked warmly of the old days to a group of people who gathered around him. As the evening progressed, he grew quiet, but seemed to scrutinize everybody with a strange intensity. When Virginia suggested they leave, he agreed but kept looking back, and when they started walking, he stopped at the crest of the hill. He stood looking down for a few moments upon the assembled guests, as if in some way he knew it was the last time they would all be together.

On September sixth when Virginia's father and mother, of whom he was very fond, were to celebrate their fiftieth wedding anniversary, he wanted to arrange a big surprise party for them. Virginia and Bob objected, fearing that it would be too much of a strain, but he insisted. The night of the party he seemed to draw upon some final reservoir of strength and laughed and talked in the way he had always managed to do at the many family parties in the past. When the last guests had gone, he chided Virginia for her concern. "Now wouldn't it have been a shame," he said, "to have missed all that fun?"

Afterwards his decline became swift and certain. His toes turned black and blue and the discoloration spread up his legs. When he tried to step on his swollen feet he cried out with pain.

On the day that he was to return to the hospital for another transfusion, Bob brought his son Chris, Galvin's oldest grandson, to show his report card to his grandfather. Galvin protested that he looked so wretched he would distress the boy and therefore should not see him. But Bob insisted that it would be a proud moment for Chris—one that he might remember for a lifetime, a moment into which he could feel he brought cheer because of the fine report. Galvin agreed and Chris was called into the room. Though the

real drama of this final meeting was hidden from
the young man, it was evident that Galvin and
Bob understood and that Galvin was moved at
the sight of the boy who marked a span of the
generations.

In the hospital, he began to run a high fever.
Then the fever receded and he felt a little better.
"How he manages to last," the nurses said.

Some strange and relentless wellspring of
spirit kept him thinking against all reason that he
would overcome this illness. The doctors knew he
would not. Helen and Burley Galvin came from
Harvard to spend their days and nights at the
hospital with Virginia. Bob traveled back and
forth from the office daily.

Most of Galvin's close friends in the company
had no awareness of the fact that he was dying.
He had been concerned that he looked so gaunt
and sick and he didn't want them to see him that
way. Now his conversations with his family were
frail straws of hope.

"I slept pretty well last night," he told
Virginia.

"That's wonderful," she said, and then in an
effort to console him, "You look better this
morning."

"The doctor was pleased too," Galvin said.
"I guess I am getting better."

His spirit and will to live communicated itself to them and even as they grieved they sought

to reinforce his resolve by being brisk and cheerful.

But alone in the room with his father, a moment of grief and loss swept Bob. "I just want you to know," he said to his father, "I love you."

"I know that," Galvin answered quietly.

On November 5, 1959, Virginia and Bob and Helen and Burley gathered beside his bed while Matt Hickey and Charley Green waited nearby. For some hours Galvin had been in a coma from which it appeared he would not rouse. Then by a slight movement of his head and his eyes he gave the impression he knew they were there. He died quietly as the priest read the prayers for the dead and a group of nuns fingered their rosaries.

*   *   *   *

The day after his father's funeral, Bob called a meeting of his top Chicago executives.

"I have had an advantage over you during these past eighteen months," he said. "It is not an advantage that I have cherished. Since the first diagnosis, though not wanting to believe, the outcome became progressively evident to me. On those less and less frequent occasions during these past eighteen months when I would hear his steps and his voice coming down the hall, I knew that for me he was no longer in the corner office.

"I gradually began to look for new sources of strength and confidence. I looked to you. What I had found was an organization that had arrived, that had matured, and had passed a test.

"But while this drama was going on, there was a greater drama going on in the corner office —a drama which, in a very special way may have been the only means of my father receiving his reward on earth as well as in Heaven. Have you ever wondered what must go on in the mind of a man over sixty years of age who has built so well and done so much good?

"Imagine if you will that my father had enjoyed excellent health from May of last year until Thursday afternoon and then that he was suddenly taken from us. He would have been actively, intimately working alongside us, doing most things for himself. Would he have seen us in the light that he did see us? Instead providence dictated that he be forced out of our midst for months and months at a time. And then his health improved. He came back into our midst for a brief period this summer and in his inquisitive way he searched the soul of the company.

"Just a few weeks ago I noted a new response from my father. Having probed here and there and everywhere, I heard him frequently say, 'You know, now we really seem to have control of this phase of our business,' or 'That guy has certainly grown and has assumed a great role,' or 'Even though this particular activity isn't rolling smoothly, I see where the fellows know how to get it back on the track.' Department after department, function after function, came under his observation.

"You gave him the greatest worldly gift of all: having served him well, you proved to him that you were ready. For that you have my undying gratitude. I believe that my father died thinking that we were ready for the task.

"Gentlemen, I know we are."

*   *   *   *

Paul Galvin's life was no mere record of facts and dates. It was a fusion of emotions and dreams that made him a man different from anyone else. What happened to him was a vital part of the adventure that he lived and he had something to learn from each day and each man.

He was not a giant with the stature of Jefferson or Lincoln, nor an inventive genius like Edison or Marconi. The journey he made in his sixty-four years on earth was not overly eventful, the saga of the small town boy building a great company in spite of despair and numerous failures was not an achievement particular to him alone.

Perhaps in his youth, he wanted the wealth and the power that many men covet. As he grew older, he placed true value where it belonged ... upon the love of his family, the affection of his friends, the respect of the men and women who worked with him each day. He would speak of these things as having the only lasting significance.

In some strange indefinable way, he influ-
enced the lives and touched the hearts of so many.
Still in conferences and meetings throughout the
company today, wherever there is still alive one
man who knew him and who remembers the kind
of man he was, the questions are asked, sometimes
aloud, sometimes to oneself, "How would P.V.
have done it?" "What would P.V. have done
here?" "Would this have pleased P.V.?" In the
buildings where his pictures still hang today, they
have a word for it. They call it the "Galvin
Touch," the little extra things with people that tie
the bow on.

His friend Matt Hickey has spoken a moving epitaph for Galvin.

"I don't know," Hickey said. "There was
something so simple about him . . . so unusual and
yet so brilliant. I have never known anybody else
just like him."

But better than anyone else Galvin captured
the essence of his own life in a commencement
address he delivered in 1953 before the graduates
of Loyola University.

"Do not fear mistakes," he said. "Wisdom is
often born of such mistakes. You will know failure. Determine now to acquire the confidence required to overcome it. Reach out . . ."

Acknowledgments

I owe a special debt of thanks to the members of the Galvin family for their generous assistance and cooperation in this biography. Through many mornings and afternoons of interviews, Robert Galvin sought and admirably succeeded in remaining scrupulously objective while helping me understand decisions in his father's life and facets of his father's character. Virginia Galvin provided me invaluable personal recollections. Helen Galvin and Raymond (Burley) Galvin made their brother's personal correspondence available to me and helped me greatly with the material on the early family years in Harvard.

The names of all the other men and women who spoke to me and helped me are far too numerous to list here although I owe them all a massive gratitude. To a few people I returned time after time for help and they have earned my heartfelt thanks. For the most part they are those who joined the company at or shortly after its founding. Elmer Wavering, Les Harder, Hank Saunders, Earl McGowan, Bill Arnos, Frank O'Brien, Vic Irvine, the late Lewis Ingram, Harry Harrison and Walter Scott. Paul Smith, historian of the company, opened his files to me and conscientiously studied the manuscript for accuracy. Fred Blakemore, editor of the *Voice,* permitted me to examine photographs and back issues of the paper. Walter Stellner, formerly a vice president of Motorola, provided me some special insight into the problems of the war years.

Outside the company, I am particularly in-

227

debted to Joe Gillies of Philco, Les Muter of the Muter Company, and Allen Williams of the DuKane Corp.

A person deserving special mention for his efforts, contributions and suggestions, during the eighteen months I worked on this book, is Allen Center, a vice president of Motorola. He helped put many events into perspective for me and, encouraging my aim of an objective biography, he opened any door I wished open and assured numerous people that they might "talk to me with complete candor and answer any question I asked."

I am also obligated to Allen Center for the services of his secretary, Marion Frangos, who typed the manuscript at least three times, who unraveled scratches and scrawls, and who coordinated appointments and travel schedules for me with an awesome competence.

All of the dialogue and events in this book are based on fact as the facts were revealed to me. But even when dealing with facts, a certain judgment is required. This judgment is solely my responsibility. How effectively I have captured the significance of the life of Paul Galvin rests on how perceptive my judgment has been.

H.M.P.

September, 1964

Index

229